Presented To:

_____

Date:

_____

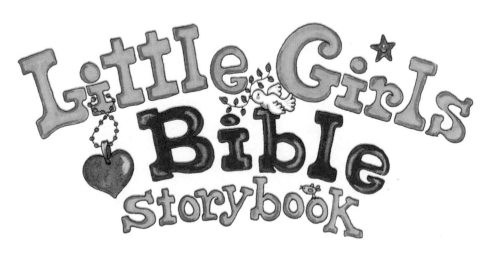

for
Mothers ♥ Daughters

Little Girls Bible Storybook for Mothers & Daughters

Published by New Kids Media™ in association with Baker Book House Company, Grand Rapids, Michigan. This edition published under arrangement with Ottenheimer Publishers, Inc.

ISBN 0-8241-0162-6

Printed in China.
SB140MLKJIHGFED

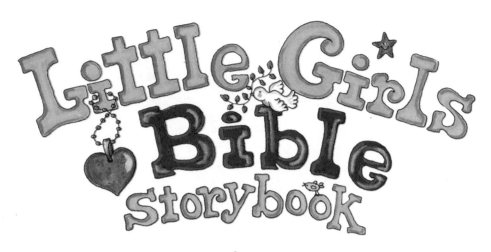

for
Mothers & Daughters

Carolyn Larsen
Illustrated by Caron Turk

Published in association with

BAKER
A DIVISION OF
Baker Book House Co

Little Girls Bible Contents

Eve's Awakening 10

The First Sin 17

Whatever You Say, Dear 24

A Rainbow Promise 31

On the Road Again 38

A Dangerous Giggle 45

Eviction 52

A Mother's Worst Nightmare 59

My Son, My Son 66

He Loves Me, He Loves Me Not 73

The Riverboat Bed 80

If God Says Go, then We Go 87

My Brother's Keeper 94

Saving the Worst for Last 101

Eating Out 108

The Perfect Ten 115

The Walls Fall Down 122

A Woman Shall Lead Them 129

A Foreigner in a Foreign Land 136

The Shame of Shames 143

The Peacemaker 150

My Baby, My Life 157

Elijah's Bread Recipe 164

Elisha's Room 171

Good Advice for Naaman 178
Esther Wins a Beauty Contest 185
We're Having a Baby 192
Big News for Mary 199
A Promise Is Born 206
My Dream Comes True 213
Wise Men from the East 220
My Son Is Lost 227
An Unusual Wedding Gift 234
The Woman at the Well 241
Longing to be Well 248
Giving My All 255
The Gift of Life 262
Daddy's Girl 269
A Mother's Love 276
A Gracious Hostess 283
Lazarus, Come Out! 290
Miracle of Mud 297
A Gift of Love 304
A Mother's Broken Heart 311
A New Day Dawns 318
"Mary" 325
A Generous Seamstress 332
New Life for Lydia 339
Sharing What You Know 346
An Angel at the Door 353

Dear Moms,

Have you ever thought about the feelings or emotions of the characters who actually lived our favorite Bible stories? The Bible doesn't often tell us what these people were thinking or feeling, so when we read these stories we may forget that they are about real people—who had struggles and questions, fears and hopes, just as we do today.

The Little Girls Bible Storybook provides an opportunity to look at well-loved Bible stories through the eyes and hearts of the women who lived them. Of course, we don't really know what these long-ago women were actually feeling, but by thinking about what they *may* have felt, we can have a deeper insight into the lessons they learned. We can learn from their experiences by imagining what a woman of today may have felt in those same situations.

Caron Turk has wonderfully illustrated these stories and I know that you will enjoy her whimsical style. You and your daughter can have fun looking for the darling little angel with the pink dotted wings who is hiding in each illustration.

My hope is that these stories will make familiar Bible characters more real to you and your daughter; and that the questions and thoughts in the *Becoming a Woman of God* section will provide some wonderful conversation starters for you and your daughter. Hopefully, you will find opportunities to tell your daughter things about your life that she may not know.

God bless you and your little girl as you read *The Little Girls Bible Storybook for Mothers and Daughters.*

Carolyn Larsen

Eve's Awakening

"Eve . . . Eve, wake up," the gentle voice whispered.

"Who is it? Who's there?" Eve mumbled, stretching her arms and wiggling her toes for the very first time.

"It's me . . . God . . . your creator. Open your eyes, sweet child. There's someone I want you to meet," God whispered again, a little louder this time.

Eve stretched again and sat up. When she opened
her eyes, she couldn't believe what she saw, "Ohhh,
it's ...it's so beautiful!" Carefully trying her brand-new
legs Eve ran through the garden, touching things for
the very first time. "What are these?" she cried,
pointing at a mound of color.

"Flowers, " God answered, "smell them."

"Mmmmm, they smell sweet!" Eve giggled.
Suddenly she glanced behind her. "What's that noise?"
she wondered, dashing across the garden.

"A waterfall," God said, enjoying her discoveries.

Eve leaned over the water and laughed out loud,
"It tickles when it splashes me," she cried with delight.

"Look, there's someone in the water!"

"No, sweet child, that's your reflection. You're looking at you," God explained. Eve tucked a strand of hair behind her ear and smiled at herself. "Come over here, child. I want you to meet Adam." Eve looked shyly at the tall man across from her.

"He looks nice," she whispered to their creator.

"He is," God smiled. "Adam, this is Eve. She will be your wife."

...And the Lord God planted a garden toward the east in Eden

"Wow, she's pretty!" Adam whispered.

"Yes, she is. And she will be a better friend for you than the animals are," God said. "She can talk and laugh—just like you do. In fact, I made you both to be a lot like me. You can talk, and think, and make decisions, just like I do. I know you'll be very happy together."

Based on Genesis 1—2

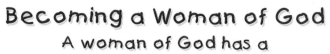

Becoming a Woman of God
A woman of God has a good self-image.

Eve was made in the image of God. That means God made her to be like him.

Are you happy with who you are or do you sometimes wish you were more like someone else— "Julie's so pretty ... Sara's so good at music ... Cori's so smart"?

MOM'S TOUCH
Share a story about something you once wished was different about yourself—and how you came to peace with it.

Then, remind yourself and your daughter that God made you both in a very special way. Take a few minutes and thank God for the specific ways he made both of you.

Help your daughter think of things that she can like about herself: She is kind to others, or she has a good sense of humor, or she is generous.

A Verse to Remember
You made all the delicate, inner parts of my body and knit me together in my mother's womb.

Psalm 139:13

The First Sin

"Pssst, hey, over here, lady!"

     With juice dripping down her chin, Eve stopped eating and looked around. Seeing no one, she took another big bite. Suddenly a shiny snake dropped its head down right in front of her. "Oh my, you scared me," Eve exclaimed. "Wait a minute, I know all the animals in the garden, but I don't recognize you. Who are you?"

And the Lord God planted
the tree of knowledge...
a garden toward the east,
in Eden...and God caused to grow

"Let'sssss just ssssay I'm a friend"

"Never mind," the snake hissed. "Why are you eating that? You could have the s-s-sweetest fruit in the garden."

"Which fruit are you talking about?" Eve asked.

"It's-s-s on that big tree in the center of the garden," the snake hissed.

"But God said not to eat that fruit," said Eve.

"Trus-s-s-st me, it's-s-s-s the s-s-s-sweetest, run-down-your-chin juiciest fruit in the whole garden."

"You make it sound so good," Eve whined.

"God didn't really mean that you s-s-shouldn't eat that fruit." The snake wrapped his body around Eve's shoulders like an old friend.

"B-b-but," Eve started to argue, but the snake led her to the big beautiful tree.

"Come on, try it!"

Eve looked at the fruit, then at the snake. Suddenly she grabbed the fruit and bit into it.

the serpent was a crafty beast......

This was a sad day for Adam and Eve

"Adam, try this!" Eve called. "It's the yummiest."

"That fruit is from the tree God told us to stay away from," Adam shouted. But he couldn't resist taking a bite of it, too.

Adam and Eve knew the damage was done. They couldn't hide their sin from God. It was hard to face his disappointment. "I'm sorry you disobeyed me. It means you have to leave this beautiful garden."

The Lord God sent Adam and Eve from the garden...

Eve cried as they left the garden, "I'm so sorry. I didn't mean to disobey—the snake made it sound so good."

"I know, child, I know. I have to punish you for disobeying, but—I still love you. I always will."

"I can take the punishment," Eve cried, "if I know that you still love me. I love you, too. I always will."

Based on Genesis 3

Becoming a Woman of God
A woman of God accepts the consequences for choices she makes.

Eve was made in God's image, but she was free to make her own choices. She made a bad choice when she chose to disobey God. God punished Adam and Eve. They had to accept the consequences of the choices they made. That means Eve had to accept the punishment for her bad choice.

When have you made a bad choice? Were you punished for disobeying?

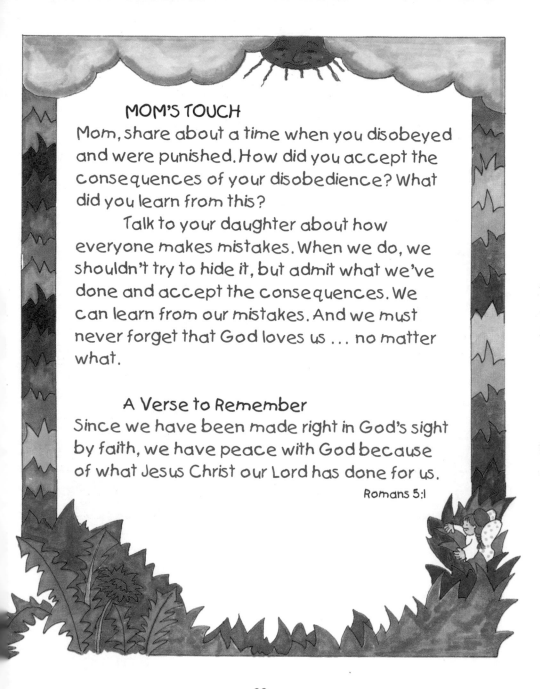

MOM'S TOUCH

Mom, share about a time when you disobeyed and were punished. How did you accept the consequences of your disobedience? What did you learn from this?

Talk to your daughter about how everyone makes mistakes. When we do, we shouldn't try to hide it, but admit what we've done and accept the consequences. We can learn from our mistakes. And we must never forget that God loves us ... no matter what.

A Verse to Remember

Since we have been made right in God's sight by faith, we have peace with God because of what Jesus Christ our Lord has done for us.

Romans 5:1

Whatever You Say, Dear

You're going to build a what?" Mrs. Noah asked.

"An ark," Mr. Noah repeated. "A boat, my dear! A big, big boat!"

"A boat? A boat? Where do you get these crazy ideas?"

"From God," Noah replied quietly.

"Gulp. Did you say God?" Mrs. Noah nervously brushed the flour from her hands as Noah explained that God was tired of the way people were behaving. It wasn't a surprise really. People had become selfish and rotten. God had tried so many times to get them to listen to him. He must have finally given up.

"God has decided to wipe out every living thing," Noah explained. "Everything on earth will die in a big flood. Then God will begin the human race again— with us."

"But we don't have any children," Mrs. Noah objected.

"You'd better start knitting booties, my dear. I think God has a plan for us," Noah smiled.

"Well," said Mrs. Noah, "if God wants you to build an ark, you'd better get busy!"

By the time the ark was built, Mrs. Noah had three sons—and they were all grown up and married.

As Noah put on the finishing touches, there was a strange clomping sound. Mrs. Noah looked up and saw a parade of animals coming toward them. "NOAH! What's going on here?" she cried.

"Um, did I mention that God is sending a few animals to go in the ark?" Noah mumbled.

"With us? We're going in the boat with those wild, smelly animals?" Mrs. Noah wondered.

"We'd better. Flood coming, you know."

Mrs. Noah looked at the lions, bears, and spiders (did there have to be spiders?) She smiled and took Noah's hand, "Whatever you say, dear."

Based on Genesis 6:1—7:9

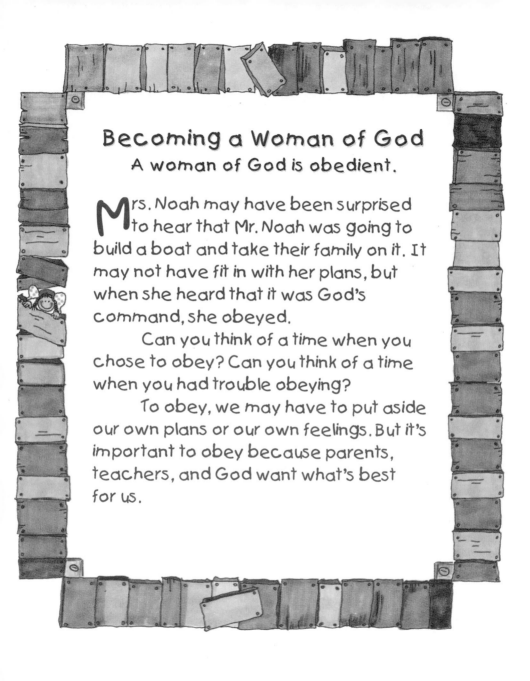

Becoming a Woman of God
A woman of God is obedient.

Mrs. Noah may have been surprised to hear that Mr. Noah was going to build a boat and take their family on it. It may not have fit in with her plans, but when she heard that it was God's command, she obeyed.

Can you think of a time when you chose to obey? Can you think of a time when you had trouble obeying?

To obey, we may have to put aside our own plans or our own feelings. But it's important to obey because parents, teachers, and God want what's best for us.

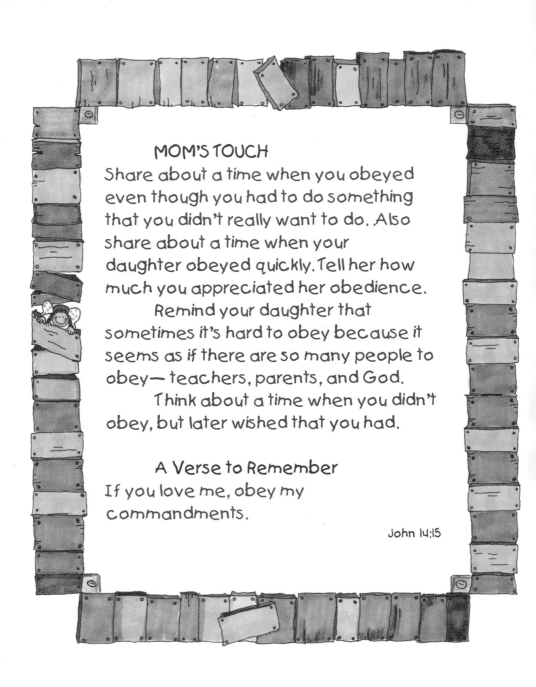

MOM'S TOUCH

Share about a time when you obeyed even though you had to do something that you didn't really want to do. Also share about a time when your daughter obeyed quickly. Tell her how much you appreciated her obedience.

Remind your daughter that sometimes it's hard to obey because it seems as if there are so many people to obey— teachers, parents, and God.

Think about a time when you didn't obey, but later wished that you had.

A Verse to Remember

If you love me, obey my commandments.

John 14:15

A Rainbow Promise

At first, the pounding of the rain was like a gentle lullaby. But soon Mrs. Noah noticed the rain was falling harder and harder and the wind was blowing fiercely. That's some storm out there! The whole earth must be covered with water by now, she thought.

Noah's family and the animals were in the ark for a long, long time. It got a little boring, (and a little stinky if the truth were told). Mrs. Noah kept busy cleaning up after the animals and keeping her family fed and the clothes cleaned.

One exciting morning, days and days after the rain had stopped, the big boat bumped against something. "Ground!" Mrs. Noah shouted, "the flood is going down and we've touched ground!" She peeked out and saw that the ark was sitting on dry ground—the very tiptop of a mountain.

She began packing up things and sweeping up the floor, getting ready to leave the boat. "I can't wait to stand on solid ground again," she cried.

Finally, Noah said it was safe to leave the ark. "Fresh air, blue sky, sunshine!" sang Mrs. Noah. She grabbed Noah's hands and danced with joy!

In the middle of their celebrating, Mrs. Noah gasped, "That's the most beautiful rainbow I've ever seen!"

"It shows my promise," God said. "I won't ever let a flood destroy the earth again. When you see a rainbow, remember my promise and how much I love you."

"Thank you for your promise," Mr. and Mrs. Noah prayed. "We love you, too."

Based on Genesis 7—9

Becoming a Woman of God
A woman of God is thankful
for God's care.

When Mr. and Mrs. Noah stepped out of the boat and saw a brand-new, shiny clean world, the first thing they did was thank God. They thanked him for his wonderful promise and for keeping them safe from the terrible flood.

When you do something helpful or nice for other people, doesn't it make you feel good when they remember to thank you?

Do you remember to thank people who do nice things for you? Do you even remember to say "thanks" for the normal things that happen every day, such as someone cooking dinner for you or driving you to soccer practice?

MOM'S TOUCH

Share some particular aspect of God's care for which you are especially thankful, such as his comfort, his guidance, or his protection.

Tell about something God has given you for which you are very thankful.

Remind your daughter of a time when she expressed thanks for something you did and tell her how good that made you feel.

A Verse to Remember

Give thanks to the LORD, for he is good! His faithful love endures forever.

Psalm 107:1

On the Road Again

Sarah packed their belongings and Abraham tied everything onto the camels. Just as she closed the last bag, her best friend came into the tent. "Sarah, you're not really leaving are you? I'll miss you so much."

"It's hard for me too, but God said that we should go—so we go," Sarah said kindly. "God promised that if we obey him, he will give us as many descendants as there are the stars in the sky!" The couple had no children and Sarah's heart ached to be a mother.

We can trust God to keep his promises

Sarah held onto Abraham's hand as they left Haran with their servants, the servants' families, and all their animals. Their friends lined the road, watching sadly. Even the little children were sad to see the kindly couple leave.

The caravan moved slowly, trusting God to lead them. "Miss Sarah, will you sing to me while we walk?"

"Of course, little one," Sarah smiled. Soon a large group of children surrounded Sarah, talking with her and listening to her songs about God's love and care.

Sarah often wished they could stop traveling and stay in one place for awhile. But she and Abraham were a team, and they tried to always obey God. Deep in Sarah's heart God's promise was still alive: Someday they would have children of their own.

Based on Genesis 12:1-9

Becoming a Woman of God
A woman of God trusts in God's promises.

God promised Abraham and Sarah that someday they would have as many descendants as there were stars in the sky. But when they were very old, they still didn't have any children.

Sometimes we have to wait a long time for God's promises to be fulfilled. Waiting is very hard to do, but waiting teaches us to trust God.

When have you had to wait a long time for a promise to be kept? What was it?

MOM'S TOUCH

Share a story about a time you trusted God and waited for something. Perhaps you were waiting for God's guidance to know what he wanted you to do.

Explain that sometimes we don't get what we pray for, but we're changed in the process.

Help your daughter understand that waiting on God is not easy. But it helps us learn to trust him. When we get impatient we can tell him how we feel and ask him to help us trust him more.

A Verse to Remember

Trust in the Lord with all your heart; do not depend on your own understanding.

Proverbs 3:5

44

A Dangerous Giggle

Sarah listened from inside the tent as the three strangers promised her ninety-nine year old husband that she would have a baby by this time next year. How long have we waited for God to keep his promise? she thought. Now he's going to keep it? Now? When I'm old and wrinkled?

As Sarah smoothed down her dress she saw her
wrinkled hands covered with bulging veins and age
spots. Suddenly the very thought of her ancient body
carrying a baby struck Sarah funny. Before she could
stop it, a deep rumbling giggle started down in her
belly and rolled up through her body until it spilled out
her mouth.

The men sitting outside with Abraham suddenly stopped talking. "Why did Sarah laugh at our news?" they asked. "Is anything too hard for God?"

"Laugh, who laughed?" Sarah defended herself. Poor Abraham looked from the men to Sarah and back again. He was completely confused.

Several months later it was obvious that the men's
message had been from God. "Abraham, I can
barely see my feet anymore!" Sarah giggled. "Oh,
come quick!" Abraham hurried to Sarah and laid his
hand on her stomach. He felt the baby growing
inside her wiggle and kick.

Nearly a year after the visit by the three men,
Abraham and Sarah became parents of a baby boy.
They named him "Isaac" which means laughter.
Sarah cradled the small miracle in her arms and
whispered, "Praise God for promises kept!"

Based on Genesis 18:1-15; 21:1-7

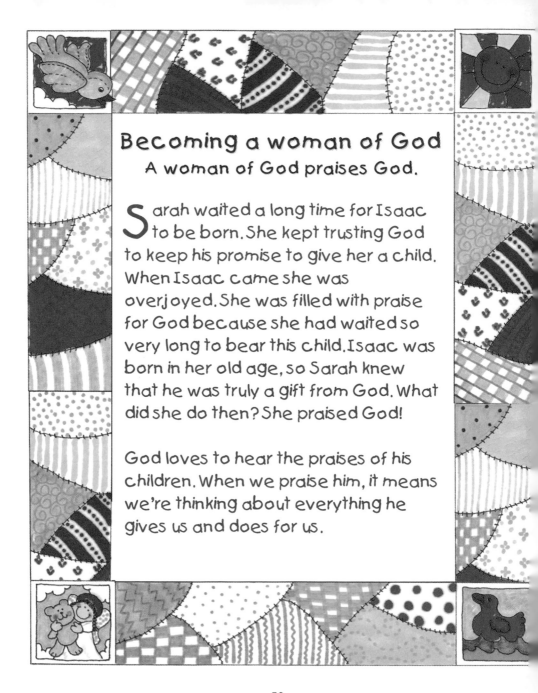

Becoming a woman of God
A woman of God praises God.

Sarah waited a long time for Isaac to be born. She kept trusting God to keep his promise to give her a child. When Isaac came she was overjoyed. She was filled with praise for God because she had waited so very long to bear this child. Isaac was born in her old age, so Sarah knew that he was truly a gift from God. What did she do then? She praised God!

God loves to hear the praises of his children. When we praise him, it means we're thinking about everything he gives us and does for us.

MOM'S TOUCH

Tell your daughter about the day you brought her home for the very first time. Did you praise God for her? Did you kiss her soft little neck and pudgy little tummy?

Share a story about a time you praised God from deep within your heart.

Everyone loves praise and no one deserves it more than God. Spend a few minutes praising him together in prayer.

A Verse to Remember

I will praise the LORD at all times. I will constantly speak his praises.

Psalm 34:1

Eviction!

Abraham remembered God's promise that he would someday have a big family. He thought perhaps Hagar's son, Ishmael, was the fulfillment of that promise. After all, he was Ishmael's father. What neither Abraham nor Hagar knew was that serious trouble was coming.

Oddly enough, the problem was Sarah, Abraham's wife. She felt that her son, Isaac, was the answer to God's promise—not Ishmael. So when Sarah saw Ishmael teasing Isaac one day, she ran to Abraham and demanded, "Get rid of that woman and her son!"

Abraham sadly gave Hagar and Ishmael food and water and sent them away. In a few days when the food and water were gone, Hagar got scared, "How am I going to take care of my son? What's going to happen to us?" Just then Ishmael started to cry, "I want to go home."

Hagar's heart broke. She walked off a little way from her son and dropped to her knees, weeping. "I don't want to watch my boy die!"

When Hagar looked up, an angel was beside her, "Don't cry. God heard your son's cries. Look, God made a well over there so you can get your son a drink. God wants you to know that Ishmael will be fine. In fact, one day he will be the leader of a great nation."

Based on Genesis 21:8-21

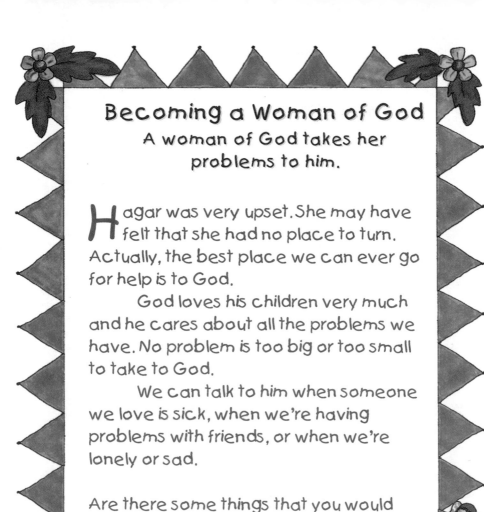

Becoming a Woman of God
A woman of God takes her problems to him.

Hagar was very upset. She may have felt that she had no place to turn. Actually, the best place we can ever go for help is to God.

God loves his children very much and he cares about all the problems we have. No problem is too big or too small to take to God.

We can talk to him when someone we love is sick, when we're having problems with friends, or when we're lonely or sad.

Are there some things that you would like to talk to God about right now? What are they?

MOM'S TOUCH

This is a good chance to show your daughter that you have problems, too, and that you take your problems to God. Tell her about some time in the past when you had a problem. Tell her how you talked to God about it. If the situation has been solved, tell her how God helped you with the problem.

A mother's love and care are so strong that her children's problems are as painful to her as her own. Talk to your daughter about how you feel when she's having a problem. Tell her how much you care and that when she's sad, you're sad, too.

A Verse to Remember

Don't worry about anything; instead, pray about everything. Tell God what you need, and thank him for all he has done.

Philippians 4:6

A Mother's Worst Nightmare

Sarah knew Abraham wasn't telling her the whole story. A wife can tell those things. When he told her that he was taking Isaac to the mountains to make a sacrifice to God, there was a catch in his throat. He just didn't sound like the Abraham she knew.

An alarm went off in Sarah's heart when Abraham and Isaac left with the wood and fire for the sacrifice—but no lamb. Sarah heard Isaac ask, "Where is the lamb?"

"God will provide, my son," Abraham answered. Sarah's heart twisted with fear as she watched them leave. Then she went inside and prayed.

The days dragged by slowly until the afternoon Sarah heard Isaac's sweet voice calling her. "Mother, wait until you hear what God did!" The story of how God took care of Sarah's precious son and blessed her wonderful husband spilled out from Isaac.

"Father tied me up and put me on the altar. I was going to be the sacrifice." Sarah's jaw dropped open as she looked at Abraham. He smiled understandingly and raised his finger to his lips before she could speak.

"Just when Father was about to . . . well, an angel of God said, 'Stop! Now I know that you fear God more than anything.' Then we saw a ram stuck in a bush. So, Father and I sacrificed it to God."

Sarah grabbed Isaac and held him tightly, more grateful than ever for God's constant love.

Based on Genesis 22:1-14

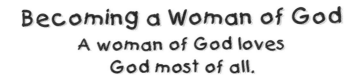

Becoming a Woman of God
A woman of God loves
God most of all.

Sarah isn't the person in this story whom we usually think of as the one being tested. But she certainly learned a powerful lesson—nothing and no one should be more important than God.

Is there anything in your life that is sometimes more important to you than God? It might be a thing or a person, or maybe it's the town where you live—you wouldn't be willing to move to a new place, even if God wanted you to.

MOM'S TOUCH

Tell your daughter how very much you love her and that you thank God every day for the privilege of being her mother.

Share about a time when you struggled with something becoming more important than God. What was crowding God out? How did you handle it?

Talk about what is important to your daughter and discuss how to keep things in proper perspective.

A Verse to Remember

You must love the LORD your God with all your heart, all your soul, and all your strength.

Deuteronomy 6.5

MY, SON, MY SON

Rebekah

Isaac

Of course Rebekah loved Esau. After all, he was her firstborn son. But Jacob was . . . special. He often helped around the house, and as they worked they talked about Jacob's dreams. So, when Rebekah heard Isaac say that he was ready to pass on the family blessing to Esau, an honor given to the oldest son of the family, a plan began to take shape in her mind.

Esau

Jacob

"I want you to get that blessing!" Rebekah told Jacob. "Whoever gets that blessing will lead the family. It must be you! Your father asked Esau to make his favorite meal before he gives the blessing. Bring me two goats and I'll cook a meal. You will take it to your father before Esau returns and you will get the blessing."

"But I ..."

"Be quiet. Just do what I tell you to do!"

After Rebekah cooked, she helped Jacob put goatskins on his arms so his skin would feel hairy like Esau's. He put on Esau's clothes and took the food to his father. Rebekah hid outside and listened. Old Isaac was blind and easily confused, "You sound like Jacob, but you feel and smell like Esau," he said.

"I am Esau, Father. Give me the blessing!" Jacob insisted.

Convinced this must be his oldest son, Isaac said, "My beloved Esau, may God bless you richly, may nations serve you, and may you rule over your brothers."

Barely able to control his joy, Jacob ran out and hugged his mother. Together they danced and celebrated.

When Esau came back, he begged Isaac for the blessing, but it was too late—once it was given, it couldn't be changed! Esau angrily vowed to get even with his brother. Jacob must leave, Rebekah thought. With her heart breaking, Rebekah watched her son go. "What have I done?" she cried. "Jacob has the blessing—that's what I wanted, but, I may never see him again."

Based on Genesis 27:1—28:6

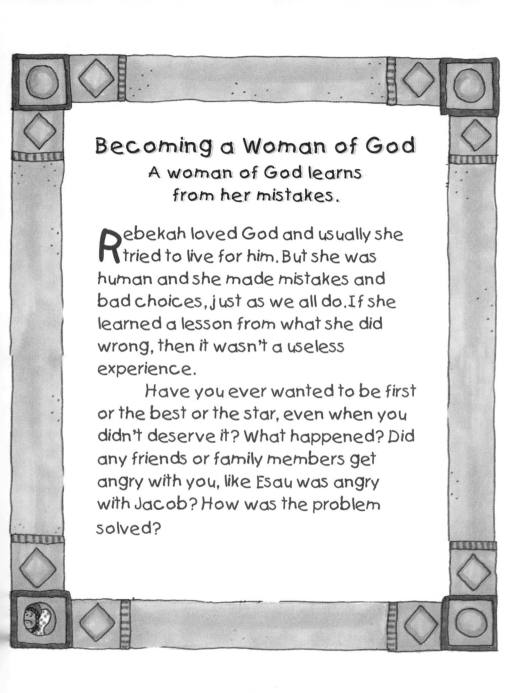

Becoming a Woman of God
A woman of God learns from her mistakes.

Rebekah loved God and usually she tried to live for him. But she was human and she made mistakes and bad choices, just as we all do. If she learned a lesson from what she did wrong, then it wasn't a useless experience.

Have you ever wanted to be first or the best or the star, even when you didn't deserve it? What happened? Did any friends or family members get angry with you, like Esau was angry with Jacob? How was the problem solved?

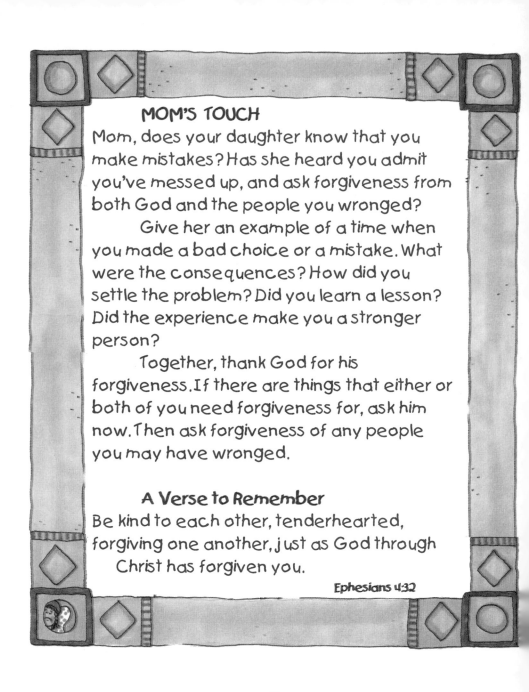

MOM'S TOUCH

Mom, does your daughter know that you make mistakes? Has she heard you admit you've messed up, and ask forgiveness from both God and the people you wronged?

Give her an example of a time when you made a bad choice or a mistake. What were the consequences? How did you settle the problem? Did you learn a lesson? Did the experience make you a stronger person?

Together, thank God for his forgiveness. If there are things that either or both of you need forgiveness for, ask him now. Then ask forgiveness of any people you may have wronged.

A Verse to Remember

Be kind to each other, tenderhearted, forgiving one another, just as God through Christ has forgiven you.

Ephesians 4:32

He loves me, he loves me not. He loves me ... Rachel plucked petals from the flower and tossed them into the wind as she thought about the young man who had recently come to live in Paddan Aram.

Jacob certainly seemed to like her, too. He looked for ways to be around her every day. Rachel was thrilled when Jacob asked her father for her hand in marriage. Jacob agreed to work for her father, Laban, for seven years and then be rewarded with marriage to Rachel.

Sometimes Rachel thought the seven years were flying by, but sometimes she thought they would never end. It was wonderful just to have Jacob close by. At the end of the day, when their work was done, they whispered and giggled and planned for their future.

But when the wedding day finally came, Rachel was crushed by her father's secret trick. "You must marry my older daughter, Leah," Laban told Jacob. "It is our custom for the older daughter to marry first."

Rachel sobbed and her beloved Jacob exploded in anger when he learned it was Leah he had married, not Rachel. "You can have Rachel, too," Laban said, "but only if you work for me another seven years."

Laban let Rachel and Jacob get married a little while later—but Jacob still had to work for Laban another seven years.

Based on Genesis 29:15-27

Seven more years....

Becoming a Woman of God

A woman of God learns that other people make choices that affect her life.

Rachel had no control over her father's choices or the customs that her family lived by. All she knew was that she loved Jacob.

Her father's decision to trick Jacob affected Rachel's life in a big way. But all she could do was wait and trust that God was in control of her life.

Sometimes life takes unexpected twists. Those can be very hard, especially if it means that plans you have had for a long time must now change.

It's important to remember that nothing surprises God. Nothing will happen to you that he doesn't know about first.

Have you ever been disappointed about changes to your plans? Did any good things happen as a result of the experience?

MOM'S TOUCH

This story involves disappointment. Rachel's wedding plans didn't go as she had imagined, so she must have been disappointed.

Tell your daughter about a time when you were disappointed about a plan you had. How did the situation develop? How did you handle your disappointment?

If possible, share how you have seen God's plan develop, even through disappointments in your life.

A Verse to Remember

Blessed are those who trust in the LORD and have made the LORD their hope and confidence.

Jeremiah 17:7

The Riverboat Bed

"I don't care what Pharaoh ordered. I can't
give him up. Just look at him, he's beautiful. I
know God has wonderful plans for my son!"
Jochebed hugged her newborn baby,
promising herself to protect him from
Pharaoh's soldiers—even though they had
orders to kill all Hebrew baby boys.

"Miriam, hold the baby and sing to him." For three months Jochebed managed to keep her precious boy a secret, but now his cries were getting stronger.

"Mother, how much longer can we hide him? Sooner or later someone will report to the soldiers that we have a baby here."

"I won't let my son die. Go to the river and pick some reeds for me. I have a plan." Jochebed worked quickly, humming to herself as she wove reeds into a small basket, then covered it with tar. Miriam held the baby and watched her mother work, wondering what on earth she was doing.

Jochebed held her son close, feeling his soft skin and enjoying his baby smell. Then she laid him in the basket, knowing she might never see him again. She carried the basket to the river and set it afloat. "Miriam stay here and keep watch," Jochebed whispered as tears crawled down her cheeks. "Please God, take care of my baby," she prayed as she slowly walked home.

Jochebed's arms ached for her son as she waited for
Miriam's report. Finally, Miriam burst into the room,
"Pharaoh's daughter found the baby. She's going to keep
him but she needs a nurse for him. Come quick! You can be
his nurse!"

"Praise God," Jochebed prayed, "for taking care of
my son!"

Based on Exodus 2:1-10

Becoming a Woman of God
A woman of God is active.

More than anything, Jochebed wanted her son to live. She believed that he should live. So, she did something about it. She did what she could and God did the rest. He took care of Moses.

There are times to wait and times to work. When you believe that something needs to be done, ask God for his help and wisdom, and then get moving!

When have you gotten involved in working on something that needed to be done? When have you not done something and later wished that you had gotten involved?

MOM'S TOUCH

When was a time you knew God was leading you to do something? Talk about how to be busy and still be open to God's leading. Talk about the ways we know God is leading us: through his Word, through our prayers, through people we respect, through our strong feelings, through opportunities we have.

Ask your daughter if she thinks God is asking her to take action about something. Ask her why she thinks this. Then pray together for the courage to act when and how God would want you to.

A Verse to Remember

Lead me by your truth and teach me, for you are the God who saves me. All day long I put my hope in you.

Psalm 25:5

Zipporah didn't know Moses well. He showed up from nowhere, on the run from Egypt. But, she soon fell in love with the kind stranger. After they married, Moses worked as a shepherd for her father. Zipporah settled into a routine and expected a normal home life to follow.

But one
day Moses
came home
with a story that
made Zipporah's heart crawl up into her
throat. "I was out in the fields and I heard
a voice. It was coming from a bush—a
bush was talking to me! And not just any
bush—a bush that was on fire. It
burned and burned, but it didn't
burn up!"

"A bush talked to you? Sit
down Moses, the sun is getting to you."
Zipporah said, trying to brush off his
story.

"Wait, it was God's voice! He asked me to do a special job for him."

At first Zipporah didn't believe Moses, but when she was finally convinced that it was God speaking to Moses, she was very proud. God asked my Moses to lead the Israelites out of Egypt, she thought. What an honor!

Zipporah worried as she began packing for the trip to Egypt. "I believe Moses can do anything he sets his mind to. But his self-confidence ... well, God had to talk him into doing this job. At least Aaron can come along to be his helper. He'll feel better if he's not alone."

Moses and Zipporah said goodbye to her family. All during the long trip to Egypt, she wondered what lay ahead. Would Pharaoh let the Israelites leave just because Moses asked him to? "Dear God," she prayed, "help my Moses. Guide his every move. Keep him safe, God … keep him safe."

Based on Exodus 3:1—4:17

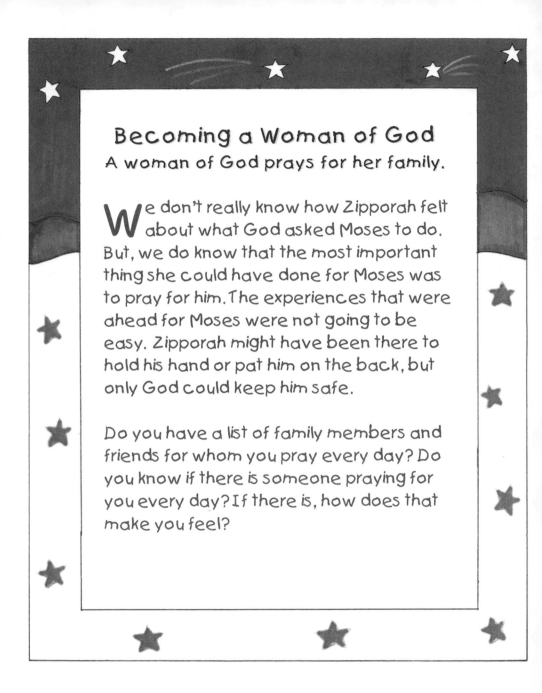

Becoming a Woman of God
A woman of God prays for her family.

We don't really know how Zipporah felt about what God asked Moses to do. But, we do know that the most important thing she could have done for Moses was to pray for him. The experiences that were ahead for Moses were not going to be easy. Zipporah might have been there to hold his hand or pat him on the back, but only God could keep him safe.

Do you have a list of family members and friends for whom you pray every day? Do you know if there is someone praying for you every day? If there is, how does that make you feel?

MOM'S TOUCH

Do you know if your mother or grandmother prayed for you when you were a child? If so, share how that was an encouragement to you.

Do you pray for your children on a daily basis? If so, share what kinds of things you pray for them. If you see your daughter growing in some of the characteristics you pray for, tell her.

Show your daughter how to start a prayer journal, keeping track of the things she prays for daily and leaving a space to record how God answers her prayers.

A Verse to Remember

Then if my people who are called by my name will humble themselves and pray and seek my face and turn from their wicked ways, I will hear from heaven and will forgive their sins and heal their land.

2 Chronicles 7:14

Miriam wiggled through the crowd. She wanted to hear everything that was being said. The angry people were shouting at her brother, "Why did you come here? Since you asked Pharaoh to let us leave Egypt, he's just made us work harder! Go away! Leave us alone!" Miriam sighed. She still had the urge to take care of her baby brother.

Miriam's heart ached for Moses. He was only doing what God told him to do and yet the people were so angry. "Trust God," Moses told them. "He wants to free you from slavery!" But the people wouldn't listen.

God is going to have to do something big to convince these people, Miriam thought.

Miriam knew that God had done something big when all the water in Egypt turned to blood. Even the Nile River!

"What will we drink? The fish are dead! Ick! It smells!" the Egyptians panicked.

Moses and God did it, Miriam thought. Now the Egyptians will know that God is boss!

But Pharaoh refused to let the Israelites leave.

Moses has to come up with something more convincing than this, thought Miriam. Sure enough, each time Moses asked and each time Pharaoh refused to let the people leave, something awful happened to the Egyptians. Frogs filled the land or gnats bugged the Egyptians, then hail killed their crops. On and on it went until nine terrible things happened to the Egyptians.

But Pharaoh was stubborn. He refused to let the Israelites leave. Miriam was amazed at her brother's total trust in God. She wondered what God and Moses would do next to get Pharaoh's attention. At least he has the Israelites attention. No one is criticizing Moses anymore, she thought. Everyone, including Miriam, waited to see what God would do next.

Based on Exodus 7:1—10:29

Becoming a Woman of God
A woman of God recognizes his power.

Miriam knew that it was God who was sending the terrible things on the Egyptians, not Moses. She may have been amazed that Pharaoh kept refusing to let the Israelites leave even though God continually showed his power.

What are some ways that you see God's power today? Can you see his power in nature? We see it in the sun, the moon, the rain and snow. It's also in the constant changing of the seasons.

How do you see God's power in people? Do you see it in peoples' attitudes and actions? Do you also see it in the miraculous way that our bodies are put together?

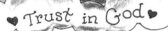
♥ Trust in God ♥

MOM'S TOUCH

Describe to your daughter a time when you were very aware of God's awesome power. Perhaps it was through the power of lightning and thunder, or through the gentle beauty of a rainbow after a storm.

Talk about how important it is for God's people to recognize his power and pay attention to him—a lesson that the Egyptians had to learn the hard way.

Make a list together of things that remind you of God's power. Talk about your favorite Bible story revealing God's power.

A Verse to Remember

O LORD, our Lord, the majesty of your name fills the earth!

Psalm 8:9

Saving the Worst for Last

Miriam hugged her oldest child as she watched her husband paint the doorframe of their house with lamb's blood. "Moses says this will keep us safe from the last plague. It's going to be a terrible one! The firstborn son in every Egyptian home will die tonight." A lump rose in Miriam's throat at the very thought. Oh, why hadn't Pharaoh just listened to Moses?

That night hundreds of Egyptian children died—even Pharaoh's son. Through his tears, Pharaoh told Moses, "Get out of Egypt."

Miriam's heart ached for the poor Egyptian mothers, as she hugged her children. A huge cloud led the Israelites out of Egypt. God was in the cloud, so the Israelites always knew he was leading them.

Finally, Moses said they should set up camp near the Red Sea. Miriam gratefully rubbed her tired feet. She longed to talk to her brother, but he was so busy. Later, she was making dinner when Miriam heard shouting. Panic gripped her heart when she saw a cloud of dust in the distance. Pharaoh had changed his mind about their freedom. His army was   chasing them!

Now what will the people do? Miriam wondered. She wasn't surprised when they got angry with Moses. "Did you bring us out here to die? Weren't there enough graves in Egypt?" How would Moses answer?

"Watch what God will do for you!"
Moses shouted. Miriam held her breath as
her brother climbed onto a rock and held
his staff over the Red Sea. Suddenly, the
waters rolled and parted into two big water
walls.

All the Israelites walked through the sea on dry ground. Miriam remembered watching Moses' basketboat on the Nile River many years before. Mother was right, she thought. God did have great plans for Moses. The last Israelite came through the sea and the Egyptians raced in, but the water crashed down on them. Every soldier died. Miriam grabbed a tambourine and sang with joy, "Praise the LORD for a wonderful victory!"

Based on Exodus 11:1—15:21

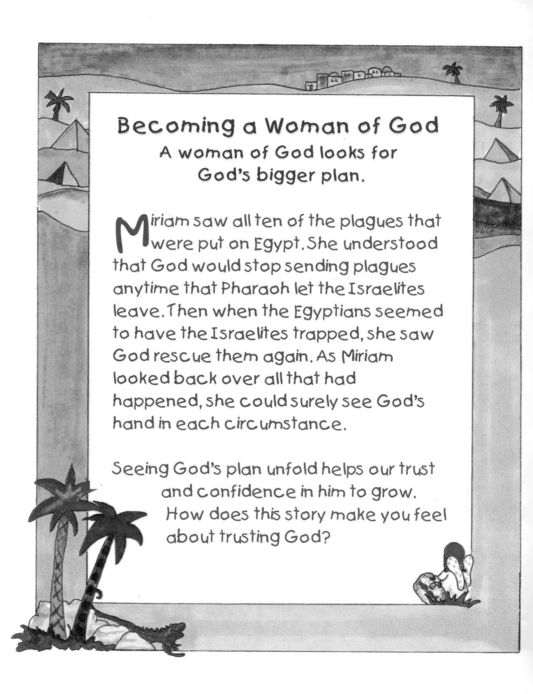

Becoming a Woman of God
A woman of God looks for God's bigger plan.

Miriam saw all ten of the plagues that were put on Egypt. She understood that God would stop sending plagues anytime that Pharaoh let the Israelites leave. Then when the Egyptians seemed to have the Israelites trapped, she saw God rescue them again. As Miriam looked back over all that had happened, she could surely see God's hand in each circumstance.

Seeing God's plan unfold helps our trust and confidence in him to grow. How does this story make you feel about trusting God?

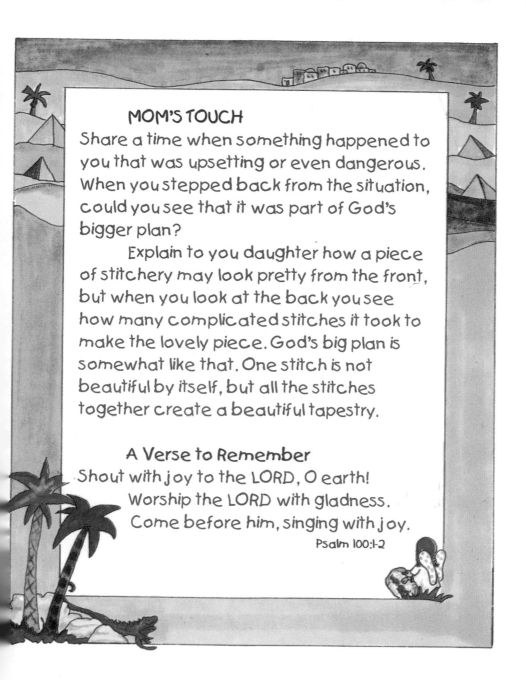

MOM'S TOUCH

Share a time when something happened to you that was upsetting or even dangerous. When you stepped back from the situation, could you see that it was part of God's bigger plan?

Explain to you daughter how a piece of stitchery may look pretty from the front, but when you look at the back you see how many complicated stitches it took to make the lovely piece. God's big plan is somewhat like that. One stitch is not beautiful by itself, but all the stitches together create a beautiful tapestry.

A Verse to Remember

Shout with joy to the LORD, O earth!
Worship the LORD with gladness.
Come before him, singing with joy.

Psalm 100:1-2

Eating Out

It seemed like everywhere the Hebrew woman went, people were complaining. "Why did Moses drag us out to this desert? At least in Egypt we had food to eat," she sighed, "I'm hungry, too. And it's hard to hear my children cry that they're hungry when I have nothing to give them."

Mostly out of curiosity, the woman went along when the people went to Moses and demanded to know what he was going to do about their problems. She was surprised to hear Moses announce, "God has heard your cries. Every morning he will give you food from heaven, and every evening he will send you meat." I want to believe Moses, the troubled woman thought, but does he know what he's talking about?

Later that day, the woman's stomach was growling when she heard an odd noise. Peeking out of her tent, she saw hundreds, maybe thousands of birds on the ground. People grabbed them and rushed to cook and eat them. Wow, she thought, this is just like Moses said. Now, I wonder what the other part of Moses' report meant.

For the first night in a very long time, the woman and her children went to bed with full tummies. It felt so good to be satisfied that the tired mother fell asleep instantly, not even thinking about the rest of God's promise. So the next morning, she was as puzzled as everyone else about the white flakes covering the ground.

"What is it?" the woman asked.

"Manna," someone answered. "It's God's gift of food to us. Taste it, it's sweet. It will make good bread."

She thoughtfully bit into the crunchy white wafer. God's gift of food . . . food from heaven. So this is what Moses meant. Thank you, God for taking care of us!

Based on Exodus 16

Becoming a Woman of God
A woman of God knows God meets her daily needs.

The woman in this story learned that God cared about her smallest needs. She, and the other Israelites, were simply hungry. God cared about their need. He helped them.

Have you thought about how God takes care of you every day? Think about all the things you do from the time you wake up each morning until you go to bed at night. Have you thanked God lately for his daily care?

MOM'S TOUCH

Have you ever been very hungry or thirsty? Has there ever been a time when you needed God to meet your basic needs of food, clothing, or shelter? Tell your daughter how God took care of you.

Perhaps you've been blessed with always having your needs met, but have volunteered in shelters or homes where people are not so fortunate. Tell your daughter how you felt in that situation.

Make a list together of all that God does for you in a single day. Post it on the refrigerator and thank him every day for his loving care.

A Verse to Remember

It is good to give thanks to the LORD, to sing praises to the Most High.

Psalm 92:1

THE PERFECT TEN

I'm tired, Zipporah thought. Since leaving Egypt the Israelites had walked for three straight months. Now they were camped at the foot of Mt. Sinai, and she just wanted to rest. Of course, when your husband is in charge of leading more than 2 million Israelites, there really isn't much chance for rest.

Moses came in just as Zipporah was lying down for a short nap. "I'm going up on the mountain," he told her.

"Now? We just got settled. Can't you rest for a while? You must be tired."

"I am tired, but God called me so I must go," Moses said.

When Moses came back, he announced that God wanted to speak to all the people. Three days later, Zipporah's heart was pounding as she stood with the other Israelites at the base of Mt. Sinai. Thunder and lightning crashed on the mountain and a thick dark cloud covered it. Zipporah could hardly catch her breath.

I wonder if this is the way God always speaks to my husband, she thought. (It was more than a little bit frightening!) Zipporah was more impressed than ever with Moses' courage and his position before God. People around her shook and trembled in fear as Moses disappeared into the cloud to speak with God alone.

- Worship God only.
- Do not make idols to worship.
- Be careful how to use God's name.
- Rest on God's day.
- Honor your father and Mother.

- Do not murder
- Keep your marriage pure.
- Do not steal.
- Do not lie.
- Do not want things that belong to others.

Days later Zipporah prayed, "God, I know you are protecting Moses, but he has been gone a long time." Zipporah admitted to herself that she would feel better when her husband was home.

When he did return, Zipporah was surprised to see that Moses was holding two slabs of stone. "They're rules," he told her. "God himself wrote ten rules for the people to live by."

Based on Exodus 18:5; 19:1—20:21

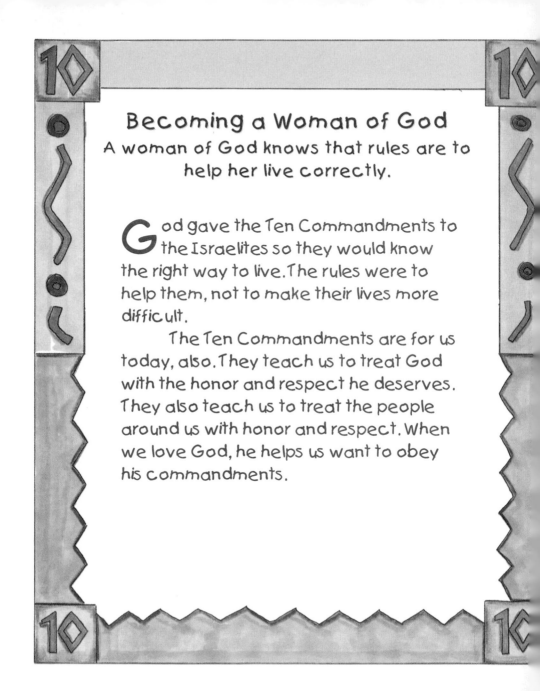

Becoming a Woman of God

A woman of God knows that rules are to help her live correctly.

God gave the Ten Commandments to the Israelites so they would know the right way to live. The rules were to help them, not to make their lives more difficult.

The Ten Commandments are for us today, also. They teach us to treat God with the honor and respect he deserves. They also teach us to treat the people around us with honor and respect. When we love God, he helps us want to obey his commandments.

MOM'S TOUCH

Tell your daughter about a time when you had trouble obeying a rule. What happened?

Ask your daughter if there are any rules she finds hard to obey. Tell her how much joy you feel when she obeys and how much sadness you feel when she doesn't obey.

A Verse to Remember

Loving God means keeping his commandments.

I John 5:3

The Walls Fall Down

Rahab was the kind of woman respectable people stayed away from. Most people pretended they didn't even see her on the street. So, she was shocked when two men came to her door. Who are these guys? she wondered. They aren't from Jericho. Rahab listened to them talking and made an interesting discovery. "They're Israelites checking out Jericho. They want to capture our city."

JERICHO

Actually, Rahab had a strong respect for the Israelites. She knew how powerful their God was. So, when soldiers came looking for the spies, she made a quick decision. "Hide on the roof. I'll get rid of the soldiers," she told the two men.

She came back to the spies and said, "I risked my life to save you, will you protect me when you capture the city?" The spies agreed and gave her a red rope to hang in her window so they would be able to find her quickly.

The Israelite army arrived a few weeks later. Rahab packed her things and waited to be rescued. But for six days the Israelites just silently marched around the city—once a day. What are they doing? Why don't they just attack? Rahab wondered, getting more nervous each day. The Israelites kept on marching.

On the seventh day the Israelites began their daily march. But they didn't stop after marching once around the city. They marched around and around. This must be the day, Rahab thought. She didn't even realize she was so nervous that she was holding her breath. Suddenly, the priests blew their horns and the Israelites shouted! Rahab screamed! The huge walls around Jericho began to crumble and fall.

...and the walls came a tumbling down....

JERICHO

Dust and screams filled the air as Rahab fell to her knees and prayed, "O Israelite God, please let the spies remember their promise." Just then a soldier grabbed her arm.

"Are you Rahab?" he shouted. She nodded and he said, "Come on, you've got to get out of here."

They remembered! "Thank you, God," Rahab prayed, "You are an awesome God."

Based on Joshua 6

Becoming a Woman of God
A woman of God chooses God even when those around her do not.

When the spies first came to Jericho, Rahab might not have believed in God. But she had heard of the awesome things God had done to protect his people. She respected his power and chose to let his power protect her instead of destroy her. The other people in Jericho had surely heard the same stories, but they had chosen to ignore them and we know what happened to them!

Do you ever feel like the only one in your group of friends who cares anything at all about God? How can you gently show others by your life that God is important to you?

MOM'S TOUCH

Almost every Christian has met someone who makes fun of their faith or gives them a hard time about it. Share a time when you chose God even though those around you didn't. How did you feel? Were you scared? Lonely?

Assure your daughter that it's OK to not always go along with the crowd, especially if that means denying her faith in God.

Pray together that God will give you both the courage to live for God each day.

A Verse to Remember

What does the LORD your God require of you? He requires you to fear him, to live according to his will, to love and worship him with all your heart and soul.

Deuteronomy 10:12

How many times will God have to rescue my people from their foolishness? Deborah wondered. The Israelites had often turned away from God and then begged for his help when they were in trouble. Jabin's army had been beating up on them for twenty years now. And here were the Israelites ... begging God to help them ... again.

Deborah was a prophetess. She gave God's word to the people. It was a big job, especially because the people hardly ever listened to God's words. Many people brought their problems to her and she patiently told them what they should do. Then one day God told Deborah his plan for freeing the Israelites from Jabin.

Deborah immediately told Barak, "God says to take your army to Mt. Tabor. God will bring Sisera, Jabin's army commander there. You can capture him!" Deborah bubbled with excitement.

But, Barak's response shocked her, "I will only go if you go with me!"

"What?" Deborah shouted. "If I come, a woman will get the credit for this victory, not you!"

Barak didn't care. He wanted Deborah with him.

It was a frustrated Deborah who marched up Mt. Tabor with Barak and his ten thousand men. Deborah and Barak saw the cloud of dust as Sisera and his nine hundred iron chariots approached. Deborah eagerly waited for Barak to command his army to attack, but he didn't. "Go on," she finally shouted. "God brought Sisera to you. Capture him!"

Deborah's words pushed Barak into action and the battle began. But Sisera deserted his army and ran off to save his own life. Just as Deborah had predicted, the honor of defeating Sisera and freeing the Israelite people went to a woman. A woman named Jael killed Sisera while he was sleeping. Deborah celebrated the victory with a song of praise to God!

Based on Judges 4—5

Becoming a Woman of God
A woman of God can be a leader.

Deborah had an important position in Israel. A prophetess served God by leading the people and fighting against their enemies. She must have been a very strong woman.

Deborah's job probably wasn't easy, but she knew it was important for the Israelites to defeat their enemies, so she did what she needed to do to make that happen.

Do you like leading, or would you rather be back in the crowd? Have you ever been the leader in getting your group of friends to do something? What was it?

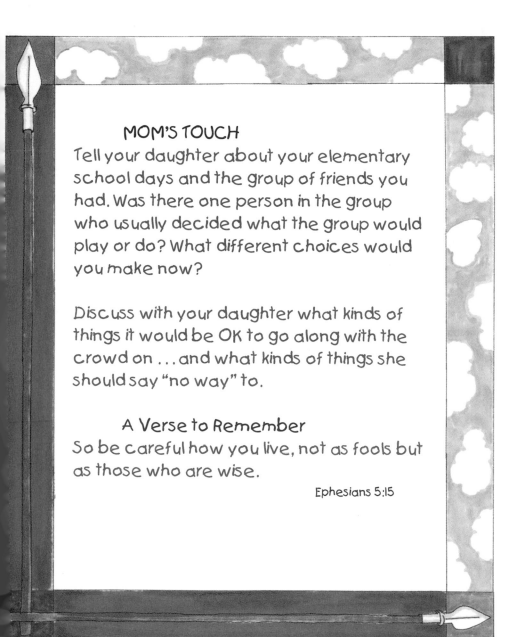

MOM'S TOUCH

Tell your daughter about your elementary school days and the group of friends you had. Was there one person in the group who usually decided what the group would play or do? What different choices would you make now?

Discuss with your daughter what kinds of things it would be OK to go along with the crowd on ... and what kinds of things she should say "no way" to.

A Verse to Remember

So be careful how you live, not as fools but as those who are wise.

Ephesians 5:15

Ruth's husband was from another country. He didn't know her ways and she didn't really know his. All Ruth knew was that she loved him. He was a nice man whose family had moved to Moab because there was no food in their land. His widowed mother, Naomi, was sweet to Ruth and her sister-in-law, Orpah.

A FOREIGNER IN A FOREIGN LAND

Ruth had never dared to dream she could be so happy. It was almost too good to be true. But one dark day everything changed. Ruth's and Orpah's husbands died. Both of them. Ruth's heart ached so much that she thought it would break. Ruth, Orpah and Naomi cried together for their dead husbands.

Ruth didn't think things
could get any worse, until Naomi decided to return to
Judah. "I won't let you go alone," Ruth declared. Orpah
came along, too.

But soon after they began the trip, Naomi said, "Go
home, girls. You're young, you can marry again. Go home
to your people." Orpah did go back home. But Ruth
promised to stay with Naomi.

Once Ruth and Naomi got to Judah, they had no job and no money. They often didn't know where their next meal was coming from. Then Ruth took charge. She went to a grain field that belonged to a man named Boaz. Ruth picked up any grain left on the ground by the workers.

"Boaz is a nice man who treats his workers kindly," Ruth reported to Naomi.

"Ruth works hard and is very loyal to Naomi," Boaz's friends told him. Soon Boaz and Ruth married and had a baby boy. Their son would be an ancestor of Jesus Christ.

Based on the Book of Ruth

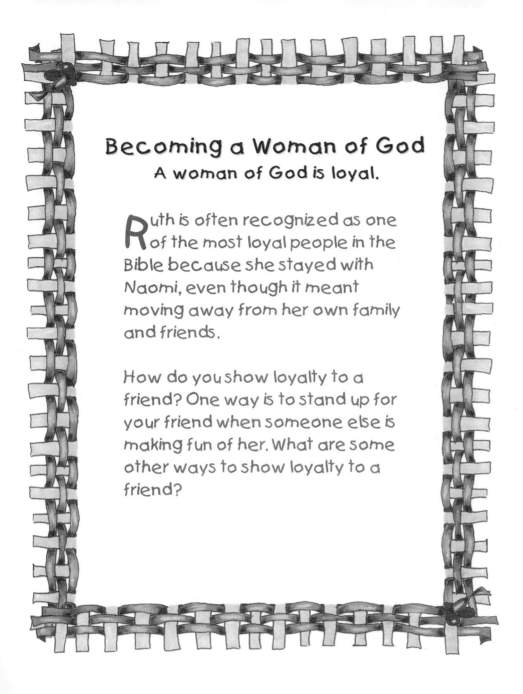

Becoming a Woman of God
A woman of God is loyal.

Ruth is often recognized as one of the most loyal people in the Bible because she stayed with Naomi, even though it meant moving away from her own family and friends.

How do you show loyalty to a friend? One way is to stand up for your friend when someone else is making fun of her. What are some other ways to show loyalty to a friend?

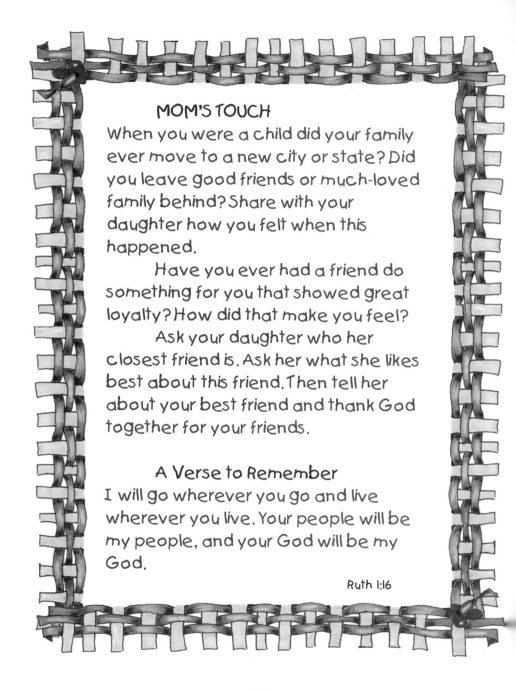

MOM'S TOUCH

When you were a child did your family ever move to a new city or state? Did you leave good friends or much-loved family behind? Share with your daughter how you felt when this happened.

Have you ever had a friend do something for you that showed great loyalty? How did that make you feel?

Ask your daughter who her closest friend is. Ask her what she likes best about this friend. Then tell her about your best friend and thank God together for your friends.

A Verse to Remember

I will go wherever you go and live wherever you live. Your people will be my people, and your God will be my God.

Ruth 1:16

The Shame of Shames

"Useless! That's what you are. What good is a wife who can't give her husband a child!" Peninnah constantly insulted Hannah. They had the same husband but the two women definitely did not like each other. Peninnah seldom missed an opportunity to brag that she had several children but Hannah did not have even one child.

"Hannah, I love you. It doesn't matter to me that you have no children," Elkanah often tried to comfort her. But the cry deep in Hannah's heart could not be silenced. Of course, Peninnah made sure that Hannah was constantly reminded of her failure to have a child.

One year, Elkanah and Hannah went to Shiloh to worship God at the temple. Hannah's heart was filled with sadness as she knelt at the altar. "Please God," she sobbed. "Please see how very miserable I am. God, I promise that if you will bless me with a child, I will give him back to you, to serve you."

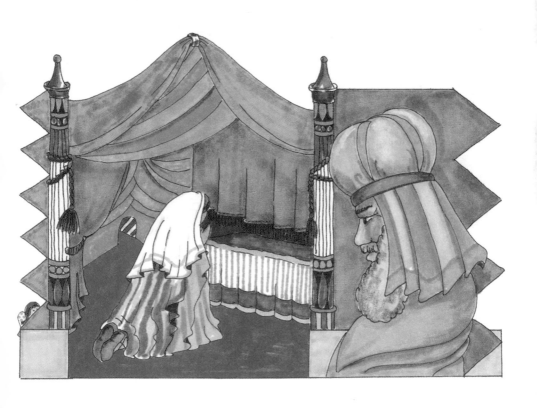

Eli, the priest, was watching Hannah at the altar. Her lips were moving but he could hear no sound. Eli didn't know the pain in Hannah's heart or the honesty of her prayer. "What do you mean by coming to God's temple when you are so drunk that you don't make sense?" he scolded her.

"I haven't been drinking. I have been pouring out my heart, begging God to give me a baby," Hannah told Eli.

Some time later Hannah did have a baby—a son whom she named Samuel—which means "Because I asked the Lord for him." Hannah remembered her promise to God; so when Samuel was old enough, she took him to live with Eli at the temple. Samuel helped Eli and learned to serve God. Hannah came to visit Samuel once a year and brought him a new robe.

Based on 1 Samuel 1

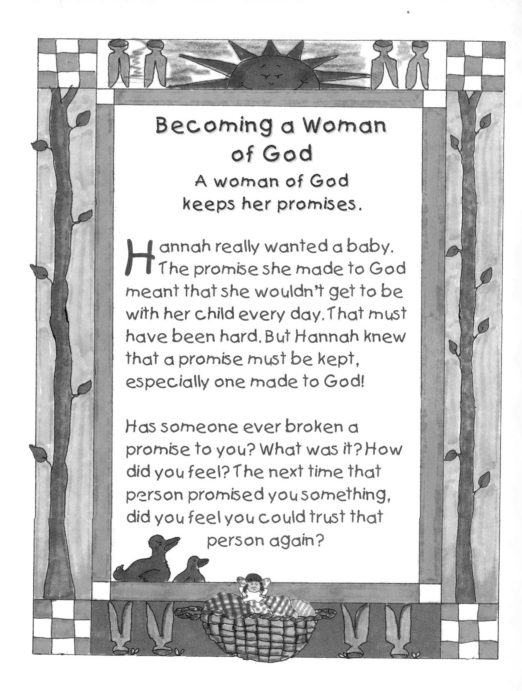

Becoming a Woman of God

A woman of God keeps her promises.

Hannah really wanted a baby. The promise she made to God meant that she wouldn't get to be with her child every day. That must have been hard. But Hannah knew that a promise must be kept, especially one made to God!

Has someone ever broken a promise to you? What was it? How did you feel? The next time that person promised you something, did you feel you could trust that person again?

MOM'S TOUCH

Do you love being a mom? Tell your daughter how you felt when you found out you were going to be a mother. Do you understand how much Hannah wanted to have a child?

Talk to your daughter about how important it is to keep promises. Give her some examples from your life of promises kept or promises broken and what the results were.

Discuss with your daughter what kind of promises people make to God. Why is it important to keep promises made to God?

A Verse to Remember

The LORD hates those who don't keep their word, but he delights in those who do.

Proverbs 12:22

"Stubborn fool...he is so rude...makes people so
angry. I'm tired of covering up his stupidity!" Abigail
tossed food into baskets as quickly as her hands would
move, all the time complaining about her husband,
Nabal. She was right. Nabal was rude and mean. And
this time, Nabal had gone too far.

"I don't know if I can help him out this time. He has made David angry. King David!!!! Everyone knows about David—I mean we sing songs about his victories. He's our hero!

"All David wanted was a little food. It wouldn't have been hard for Nabal to give him food for his soldiers. After all, while they camped by us last year, we didn't have a single problem."

"But no—Nabal makes a nasty comment about why should he give his food to a lousy band of outlaws. Oh my, David is going to kill him. He's just going to kill him."

Abigail finished packing bread, wine, meat, grains, raisin cakes and fig cakes. She carried the baskets outside and tied them on donkeys. Then she climbed on a donkey and headed down the dusty road toward David's camp.

"I wish this donkey would walk faster," Abigail sighed. But a few minutes later, she looked up and saw David and his men coming up the hill—on their way to kill her husband.

When David got closer, Abigail called out, "Sir, my husband is a fool. I accept responsibility for what Nabal did. I didn't know about your request until it was too late, so I've brought you some food now."

"Sir, you've never done anything wrong in your whole life. Don't start now. Don't murder my husband, please forgive him," Abigail begged.

Abigail breathed a sigh of relief when David thanked her for stopping him from doing something wrong. She went home praising God that David had heard her pleas!

Based on 1 Samuel 25:1-35

Becoming a Woman of God
A woman of God is a peacemaker.

Abigail knew that her husband was in trouble. She came up with a plan and went out of her way to make peace with King David.

How do you feel when you are around people who are fighting or arguing? It's not much fun is it? Have you ever tried to be a peacemaker and get your friends or family members to make up?

Has a friend tried to be a peacemaker for you? What do you think of Abigail's plan of taking gifts to give David in order to make peace?

MOM'S TOUCH

When have you been a peacemaker? Have you ever been a peacemaker between your children? Can you give an example to your daughter? Ask her if she has ever been a peacemaker.

Discuss with your daughter some of the words a peacemaker can use, such as, "When you say that it makes me feel...", "I really like it when you do ...but, when you do ... I feel bad."

A Verse to Remember

How wonderful it is, how pleasant, when brothers live together in harmony!

Psalm 133:1

MY BABY, ♥ MY LIFE

King Solomon's incredible wisdom was known around the world. It was a gift from God which the king used to help his people. That's why the sad mother went to Solomon with her problem. Her heart was filled with panic and the woman truly believed that the king was her last hope.

The woman bowed before King Solomon. A second woman entered, holding a small baby in her arms. The first woman pointed to her and said, "We both had little babies. During the night her baby died, so she took my live baby and laid her dead baby beside me. This morning I was very upset when I thought my child had died."

"NO!" screamed the other woman. "She's lying. This live baby is mine and the dead one is hers!"

Solomon looked at both women as he thought about what to do. Suddenly he ordered his servant, "Bring a sword. Cut this child in two and give half to each woman!" For a brief moment time seemed to stop. Neither woman dared to breathe.

"No!" the first woman screamed. "Don't hurt him. Let her have him." She fell on the floor, unable to stop crying.

At the same time the second woman held out the baby. "Fine!" she shouted. "Kill him! If I can't have him, then neither can she!"

King Solomon seemed to smile, as if he knew a secret. "Stop. Give the child to the first woman. She is his mother," he said.

The sobbing woman looked up, "H-H-How did you know?" she whispered.

Now King Solomon did smile, "Because the real mother would rather give up her child than let him be hurt." The woman hugged her child, knowing deep in her heart that the king's wisdom was truly a gift from God.

Based on I Kings 3:16-28

Becoming a Woman of God
A woman of God sacrifices for her children.

The true mother of the child loved him so much that she was willing to give him up rather than have him be hurt or killed. She cared more about her child's safety than about her own desires.

What are some ways that your mother and father sacrifice their own desires or plans for you? Don't answer too quickly—think about things like how much time they spend driving you to music lessons or sports practices.

Do you know that Mom and Dad are showing their love for you by the things they do for you?

MOM'S TOUCH

Explain how much you love your child. Explain how the sacrifices you make with your time, money, and interests are because you want your child to be happy and to have chances to try many different things.

Hug your daughter and tell her how much you love her. Tell her how you pray for her every day.

A Verse to Remember

Teach your children to choose the right path, and when they are older, they will remain upon it.

Proverbs 22:6

I'm so tired. If I could just sit down, the woman thought. For days she had skipped meals so her son would have food to eat. The woman's thoughts wandered to memories of when her husband was alive. Back then their dinner table was full—bread, meat, vegetables, and sweet cakes for dessert. She could almost smell the food, until her thoughts were interrupted.

A man's voice surprised her, "Excuse me, could I possibly have a drink of water?" She looked up to see Elijah, a prophet of God standing there. The woman laid down the sticks she had been gathering and reached to get him a cup of water. "I could use a bite of bread, too," Elijah added. She choked back tears, knowing that she couldn't help him.

The woman looked over at her precious son. Her heart was filled with love for him, but fear of the future. "I wish I could help you," she whispered to Elijah. "But there isn't a bite of bread left in my house. I was just gathering sticks to cook up the little bit of flour and oil I have into a small loaf of bread. When that's gone, my son and I will starve to death."

The woman thought she was hearing things when Elijah said, "Don't worry about this. Go ahead and bake your loaf of bread. But make a small one for me first. You'll have plenty of flour and oil." The woman didn't have the strength to argue.

Surprisingly, after she had baked a small loaf for Elijah flour and oil were still left in her jars. She made food for herself and her son and again flour and oil were left over. The woman slowly regained her strength, all the time praising God because her flour and oil never ran out. "God is good. He has taken care of me and my son!"

Based on I Kings 17:8-16

Becoming a Woman of God
A woman of God believes God has a plan.

The woman in this story did what Elijah told her to do, even though she knew that she was out of food. God rewarded her by continuing to give her flour and oil.

Sometimes it's hard to do what you're asked to do because you just can't see the point of it. It doesn't seem like doing that particular thing or obeying a certain request will change the way things are.

What hard things have you been asked to do? Why were they hard? Did you do them?

MOM'S TOUCH

Sometimes when we are going through a difficult time, it's hard to see that there is a bigger plan taking shape. Share examples from your past of how God's plan developed through a series of circumstances.

One good way to see how God's big plan is in constant motion is through looking back at our lives and seeing how God has led us or protected us. We can also look at the Old Testament stories of how God protected the Israelites.

Talk about different ways to get through hard times, such as praying about them, talking to Mom and Dad, or talking to a friend.

A Verse to Remember

The LORD is my shepherd; I have everything I need.

Psalm 23:1

The kind woman from the little town of Shunem took
great pride in the fact that her house was always
neat and clean. She had enjoyed decorating her
home and she loved sharing it with others. The little
woman was known throughout Shunem for her
hospitality and kindness.

The gentle woman was a good cook and
generous hostess. The first time Elisha came to
town she insisted that he stay at her home. She
enjoyed having him as a guest. After all, he was
a prophet of God. Soon Elisha had an invitation
to stay at her home anytime.

After one of Elisha's visits, the gentle woman was cleaning the guest room when an interesting idea popped into her mind. Later that night she shared it with her husband, "Why don't we build on a room that will be for Elisha. Then any time he is in town he will know that he has a place to stay. He can even keep some of his things here if he wants."

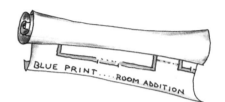

The woman's husband was surprised by her suggestion, but he was in favor of it. He made the plans immediately and the room was built and furnished before Elisha came back to town.

When Elisha knocked on her door a few weeks later, the woman welcomed him inside. She was so excited that she took his hand and pulled him through the house, "We have a surprise for you, Elisha. Look what we've made for you." Elisha was very happy. He thanked God for the kind woman and her generous husband.

Based on 2 Kings 4:8-11

Thank You God

welcome Elisha

Becoming a Woman of God
A woman of God is generous.

This kind woman in Shunem generously shared what she had to help Elisha. God is pleased when we share what he gives us, especially when we use our belongings to help his workers.

There's always a big push to help people less fortunate during the Christmas holiday season. But people need help all year long.

In what ways can you give to others? Here are some ideas: Sharing musical talent, preparing and serving food, fixing up houses, reading to older people. What else can you think of?

MOM'S TOUCH

Your children will learn generosity by watching you model it. Share ways you have been involved in generous giving, or ways that you have observed people being generous with their time and talents.

Comment on a time you observed your daughter being generous. Reinforce that characteristic in your daughter.

A Verse to Remember

Don't think only of your own good. Think of other Christians and what is best for them.

I Corinthians 10:24

Good Advice for Naaman

The little girl was really very lucky. When she was captured she became a slave to the wife of Naaman. Mrs. Naaman was very kind to the little girl. In fact, in the little girl's secret heart of hearts she thought of Mrs. Naaman in place of her own mother whom she missed so much. She often talked with the older woman, telling her about her faith in God and how much she missed her family.

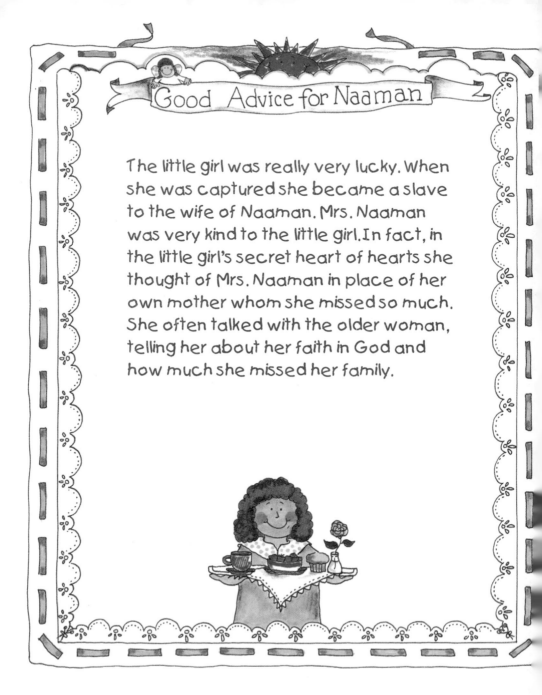

The little girl worked very hard for Mrs. Naaman and
did her work cheerfully. One day when the little girl
brought Mrs. Naaman's lunch to her, she found the
older woman crying. "Why are you crying?" the girl
asked. It was unusual that the woman would share her
own feelings with the little girl, but she was so upset
that they spilled out.

"I'm crying because my husband has leprosy. He has to leave home and live outside of town. I'm going to miss him very much."

The little girl was very sad. She liked Mr. Naaman, too. So she bravely said, "He doesn't have to leave. He can go see God's prophet, Elisha. I'm sure Elisha could help him."

The little girl seemed very sure that God would help Elisha heal Naaman. So Mrs. Naaman encouraged her husband to visit the prophet. But on the way Elisha's servant met him. "Elisha says you should go wash in the Jordan River seven times." Naaman was very angry that Elisha didn't speak to him personally, so he decided to just go home.

PRAISE GOD ♥ PRAISE GOD

But back at Naaman's house the little girl prayed with all her heart that Mr. Naaman would see God's power. When Naaman did obey Elisha and was healed, the little girl danced with joy! She had helped the Naamans in two ways: Mr. Naaman's skin was healed, and both Mr. and Mrs. Naaman knew that God's power had healed him.

Based on 2 Kings 5:1-19

Becoming a Woman of God
A woman of God can be a child.

This is a precious story in the Bible, because it shows us that even a child can lead people to God. Not only was this little girl a child, but she was also a slave. Her faith in God was so strong that she told Naaman God could heal him.

How can you share God's love with a friend? Maybe you could invite a friend to a Sunday school party or to a program at church. You could give a friend a book you like that has the message of God's love in it. Can you think of other ways to share God's love?

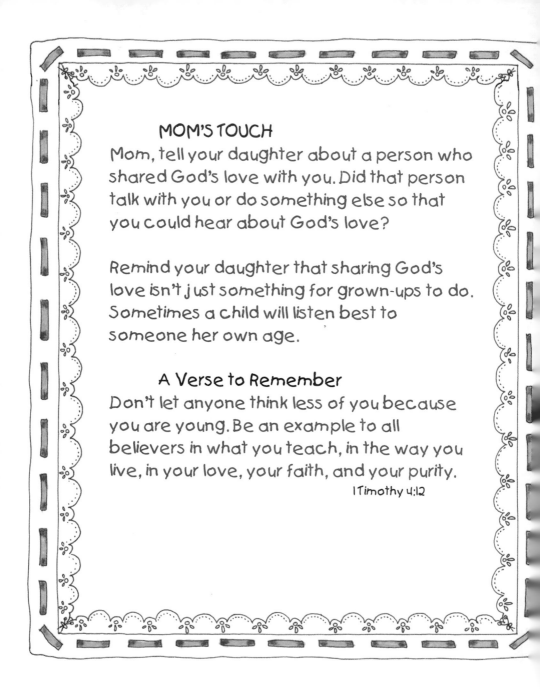

MOM'S TOUCH

Mom, tell your daughter about a person who shared God's love with you. Did that person talk with you or do something else so that you could hear about God's love?

Remind your daughter that sharing God's love isn't just something for grown-ups to do. Sometimes a child will listen best to someone her own age.

A Verse to Remember

Don't let anyone think less of you because you are young. Be an example to all believers in what you teach, in the way you live, in your love, your faith, and your purity.

I Timothy 4:12

"Esther, please help us. This may be the very reason God made you queen." Esther didn't want to hear what Mordecai was saying. She hadn't been much more than a child when she was chosen from hundreds of girls and made queen of Persia. Her great beauty and charm quickly won her the hearts of all who met her. But now the young queen was being tested.

Esther Wins a Beauty Contest

The problem started because Haman, a government leader, wanted everyone to bow down to him. One Jewish man, who happened to be Esther's uncle, refused to bow. Now Haman ordered that all the Jews in the land be killed!

"Mordecai, I can't help. No one, not even the king, knows that I'm Jewish. Remember, it was your idea for me to keep that a secret," Esther said.

"I know Dear, but all of us—including you—will die if we don't think of some way to stop Haman."

Esther went to her room and thought about the danger of going to the king when he hadn't called for her . . . he could have her killed. She wondered what he would think when he found out she was Jewish. She thought about all the dangers and choices. Then she sent a note to Mordecai. I'm going to talk to the king. Pray for me—if I die, then I die.

Esther put on her prettiest dress and
splashed on some perfume. Then she
invited the king and Haman to a special
dinner. They were enjoying the food and
laughing and talking when Esther found
the courage to say, "Haman is planning
to kill me and my relatives!"

Haman nearly choked as Esther explained his whole evil plan and her own Jewishness. Esther breathed a deep sigh of relief as soldiers led Haman away. King Xerxes had him hung on the gallows which Haman had built to kill Mordecai. The Jews were saved, thanks to the courage of a beautiful, brave young queen.

Based on the Book of Esther

Becoming a Woman of God
A woman of God takes a stand for him.

Wasn't Esther brave? The king could have ordered that she be killed because she came to him without being called—or because she was Jewish. Even if Esther was very scared, she knew she had to stop Haman.

Have you ever wanted to stand up for God when other kids were making fun of him? Have you ever heard kids saying mean things about someone else? Did you try to stop them? It's not easy to go against the crowd, is it?

MOM'S TOUCH

Share a story about some injustice that once bothered you (or currently troubles you), even if you have done nothing about it.

If you have taken a stand for God or another person, share that story. Were you scared? What was the outcome?

Discuss with your daughter that taking a stand for God might mean explaining why she goes to church or Sunday school. It might mean explaining why she prays before she eats lunch. Encourage her to give her explanations in gentleness and love. And remind her that she never has to take a stand alone—God will help her!

A Verse to Remember

For I can do everything with the help of Christ who gives me the strength I need.

Philippians 4:13

We're Having a Baby

Elizabeth shook her head in frustration. "What are you trying to tell me? Why don't you just talk?"

Her husband, Zechariah was just as frustrated as she was. Finally, he picked up a stick and wrote in the dirt, "We're going to have a baby."

Elizabeth read the words ... then read them again. "A what? A baby? Do you know how old ... have you lost your mind?"

Zechariah quickly scribbled another word in the dust: Angel. At first Elizabeth didn't understand ... it had been years since he had called her his "angel" so he must mean that he had seen an angel. Sure enough, through his scribbles Elizabeth learned that an angel had come to her husband and said that they would have a baby boy and that they must name him John.

Their son would prepare the world for the coming Messiah. What an honor! She also found out why Zechariah was drawing signs in the dust instead of telling her this miraculous news. He had doubted the angel's message so the messenger from God had taken his voice away until the baby was born. After hearing that, Elizabeth was careful not to question another bit of Zechariah's news.

At the oddest moments Elizabeth would rub her hand
across her stomach and think, A baby. I'm going to
have a baby. She and Zechariah had prayed for a child
for years. But she had given up hope, thinking her
withered old body was too old to carry a child. Joy
bubbled up inside her as she thought, Well, I surely won't
argue with God about this.

Nine months later, relatives gathered with Zechariah and Elizabeth to celebrate the birth of their son. Elizabeth cradled the child in her arms. Aunts and uncles argued back and forth with name ideas while Zechariah peeked over the crowd at Elizabeth. He raised a stone tablet in the air with big words scratched on it, "His name is John."

Based on Luke 1:5-25, 57-63

Becoming a Woman of God
A woman of God enjoys God's surprises.

Elizabeth and Zechariah must have thought their lives were all settled. They were old now and had never had children. Zechariah was busy with his work, and Elizabeth kept busy with the house and her friends.

Wow, did God give them a special surprise! He gave them a baby in their old age. When God is involved, nothing is impossible!

Is there something you have prayed about for a long, long time? What is it? Have you given up on God ever answering that prayer? Do you still pray for it?

MOM'S TOUCH

Help your daughter understand Elizabeth's emotions by explaining what it's like physically to have a child growing inside you. Maybe you, like Elizabeth, longed for a child but were unable to have one. Discuss with your daughter how God answered your prayer for a child.

Ask your daughter to describe the best surprise she ever received. Then tell her about a way God once surprised you. Spend a few minutes together in prayer, thanking God for his surprises.

A Verse to Remember

Keep on asking, and you will be given what you ask for. Keep on looking, and you will find. Keep on knocking, and the door will be opened.

Matthew 7:7

Big News for Mary

Mary dragged the heavy wooden bucket into the house. The daily trip to the town well for the family's water was tiring. She was glad to sit down in the cool darkness of the house for a minute of rest. Leaning her head against the wall, Mary's thoughts drifted to wedding plans and her handsome fiancé, Joseph. He was a carpenter and a gentle, patient man.

I'd better get back to work, Mary thought. Suddenly she realized that she wasn't alone. "Oh, I didn't hear you ...." Something about the stranger made Mary's words catch in her throat.

"Hello Mary," he said. "Congratulations, you are a very blessed woman. God is with you." Mary's mouth dropped open as she realized that the stranger was an angel sent from God.

The angel continued speaking and Mary grew more frightened with each word he spoke. "Don't be afraid, Mary. I've come to tell you that you are going to have a baby." Mary backed away from the angel, until she bumped against the cold stone wall.

"I-I-I can't have a baby," she whispered. "I'm not even married..."

"I know, but your baby will be God's son," the angel said. "You are to name him Jesus. His kingdom will never end!"

Mary's eyes grew as big as saucers and she nervously walked around the room. She had never felt so confused ... or frightened ... or honored. What would Joseph say? What would her family say? Had God really chosen her?

Mary stared into the angel's face and he waited for the incredible news to sink in before reminding her, "Nothing is impossible with God, Mary."

Mary closed her eyes and took a deep breath before saying, "I am God's servant. I will do whatever he wants me to do!" When she opened her eyes, the angel was gone.

Based on Luke 1:26-38

Becoming a Woman of God
A woman of God is chosen by God.

Mary was chosen for a great honor. But God didn't choose her because she was pretty or because she sang well or because she was from the right family. He chose her because she loved God and wanted with all her heart to please him.

Have you ever been chosen for something? It feels good to be chosen for a team or chosen to be in a play. It feels good to be chosen for anything—especially if you know that you have earned the honor.

MOM'S TOUCH

Tell your daughter about a time you were chosen to do something or be in something. How did it feel to be chosen for this? Why were you chosen? Did it give you added responsibility? Were your friends happy for you or jealous of you?

Talk to your daughter about how God has chosen us to be his children. Talk about what it means to be in God's family.

A Verse to Remember

For his Holy Spirit speaks to us deep in our hearts and tells us that we are God's children.

Romans 8:16

A PROMISE IS BORN

Mary's large tummy promised
that her baby would be born
very soon. Taking a bumpy donkey
ride was the last thing she should be
doing. But since her baby could be
born any day, she didn't want to be
away from Joseph. If only we didn't
have to go to Bethlehem for that silly
census, she thought.

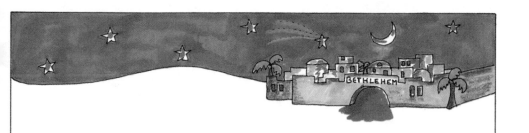

"Are you OK, Mary?" Joseph asked again. She told him she was fine, but truthfully, Mary had never been so exhausted. Only sheer willpower kept her on the donkey. The baby kicked harder with every step the donkey took. "This baby is trying to kick his way into the world," she sighed.

"Hang on, Mary, we're almost there. We'll get a nice room in Bethlehem," Joseph promised.

Mary was not prepared for the crowded, noisy streets of Bethlehem. She waited wearily for Joseph to get a room at the inn, trying not to be sickened by the smell of sweaty bodies and dirty animals. Joseph returned with bad news.

"There are no rooms, Mary. The innkeeper says the whole town is full. Since you're pregnant he said we could stay in his stable. I'm sorry, Mary," Joseph apologized.

"It's OK, Joseph. I just want to lie down."

Mary slid from the donkey to the mound of straw Joseph had gathered. She was asleep instantly. Sometime after dark Mary was jolted awake by a sharp pain grabbing and twisting her stomach. "Joseph, wake up ... the baby!"

Pain roared through Mary's body. Joseph tried to comfort her. But it was only when he pulled the baby from her body and laid it in her arms that Mary relaxed and thanked God for letting her share in this incredible miracle.

Mary washed her baby and counted his fingers and toes. She was overwhelmed with love for him, yet barely dared to think about who he really was. However, the truth slammed into Mary's heart when she looked up to see some scraggly shepherds peeking over the stable door. "We saw an angel...special baby born...our savior," their words swam in Mary's mind. Softly, her heart began to sing, "My baby, my savior...I'm holding God in my arms."

Based on Luke 2:1-20

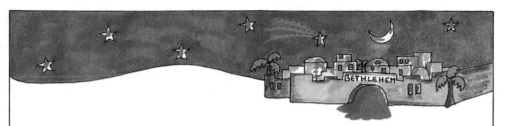

Becoming a Woman of God
A woman of God does the work of God.

The work that Mary did for God was not just a great honor, it was also very difficult. Sometimes the work of God is very hard, but the end result is wonderful and exciting. Doing God's work gives us great joy.

Do you have chores to do at home? It pleases your parents when you do your chores and do them well. What kind of work do you enjoy doing? What kind do you not enjoy doing?

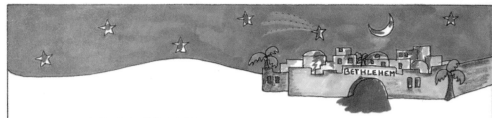

MOM'S TOUCH

Mom, what kind of work do you do for God? Take care of your family? Sing in the choir? Teach Sunday School? Work with children? Volunteer in a nursing home?

Share with your daughter the ways that you work for God. Help her see that working for God doesn't require being able to quote lots of Bible verses or teach big classes. It simply means using the interests and abilities God gives us.

Talk to your daughter about what she can do for God. What are her interests and abilities? Pray together, telling God you both want to do things for him and asking him to show you ways to serve him.

A Verse to Remember

Work hard and cheerfully at whatever you do, as though you were working for the Lord rather than for people.

Colossians 3:23

My Dream Comes True

Some days it is so hard to get up and down, Anna thought as she grabbed a bench to pull herself up. Anna usually spent most of the day kneeling on the hard floor, praying to the God she loved so much. But it was getting more and more difficult to make her knees lift her back to her feet.

Anna was getting up to check on her old friend, Simeon.
She could hear him shouting. To Anna's old ears it sounded
as if he were saying, "Praise God! Now I can die a happy
man!" Anna had a lot of respect for Simeon. He spent a lot
of time in the temple, as Anna did. She knew that he was a
man of God. What on earth was he shouting about?

Anna stood still for a minute, catching her breath. Then she shuffled through the temple toward Simeon's voice. There he is, she thought. He's holding a baby in his arms, a baby! Oh, be careful, you're lifting it so high into the air. He was shouting, "Praise you, Lord. Just as you promised, I have seen the Savior of Israel, a light for the world! Now I can die a happy man."

Anna crept closer as Simeon gave the child back to his mother. They must be here to dedicate the baby to God, Anna thought. Just then she caught a glimpse of the baby's face. Anna's old heart skipped a beat—at that very moment God showed her that this baby was Messiah—the Savior that her people were waiting for.

Joy bubbled from deep inside Anna, spilling from her lips, "Praise God! Thank you for hearing the prayers of your people. Hallelujah!" Anna's wrinkled old body danced through the temple. She stopped every person she met and told them about the child. "The Savior has come. God has heard our prayers! Hallelujah!"

Based on Luke 2:25-38

Becoming a Woman of God
A woman of God recognizes her Savior.

I t's been said that when a big herd of sheep is in the field and a shepherd calls, only the sheep that belong to him will come. That's because they recognize the voice of their shepherd.

When Anna saw baby Jesus, she immediately recognized that he was her Savior. Her heart was so in tune with God that she understood who this little baby was and what he would do when he grew up.

When you are in a crowd of people and your mom or dad calls your name, can you pick that single voice out of the noise? Do you recognize that voice, even with all the confusion? Does it make you feel good to know that mom or dad is there?

MOM'S TOUCH

Tell your daughter about the first time you knew Jesus was speaking to you. Were you a child? An adult?

Ask your daughter if she has heard Jesus call her. If she hasn't, explain to her how she can learn to hear and follow the Good Shepherd.

Point out that other people saw young Jesus and thought he was just another baby. But Anna and Simeon saw him and immediately knew who he was because in their hearts they were seeking to know God.

A Verse to Remember

My sheep recognize my voice; I know them, and they follow me. I give them eternal life, and they will never perish. No one will snatch them away from me.

John 10:27-28

WISE MEN from the EAST

It had been nearly two years since Mary and Joseph came to Bethlehem. Where does the time go? Mary wondered as she washed clothes. Jesus was a good baby, but even good babies are a lot of work. Sometimes Mary missed her mom so much. It would have been nice to have her mom's help and advice, and she often wished her mom could see Jesus.

Mary glanced at Jesus playing by himself. She let her mind wander back to what the angel had said about him when his birth was announced. She remembered the shepherds' words on the night Jesus was born, and the words of Simeon and Anna in the temple. Sometimes Mary's heart grew cold with fear, wondering, "What is ahead for this sweet little child?"

Mary had made friends in Bethlehem, but she didn't talk about who Jesus really was. After all, you didn't just walk up to a neighbor and say, "By the way, did I mention that my son is the savior of the world?" Jesus looked and acted like a normal two-year-old. Mary had no idea what was going to happen in the future.

However, the day the fancy-looking strangers rode their camels right up to Mary and Joseph's little house, Mary knew the gossips in town would be very busy. She saw the crowd of people gathering outside their house. "We've come to worship the new king of the Jews," the strangers announced for the whole neighborhood to hear.

How did they find us? Mary wondered. One man answered her unspoken question, "The star led us to you." He pointed to the bright star above their house. The men knelt before Jesus and gave him the gifts they had brought. Mary's eyes grew wide when she saw the gold, frankincense, and myrrh. The men worshiped Jesus, and Mary's heart filled with joy, "Whatever happens, God, thank you for Jesus."

Based on Matthew 2:9-12

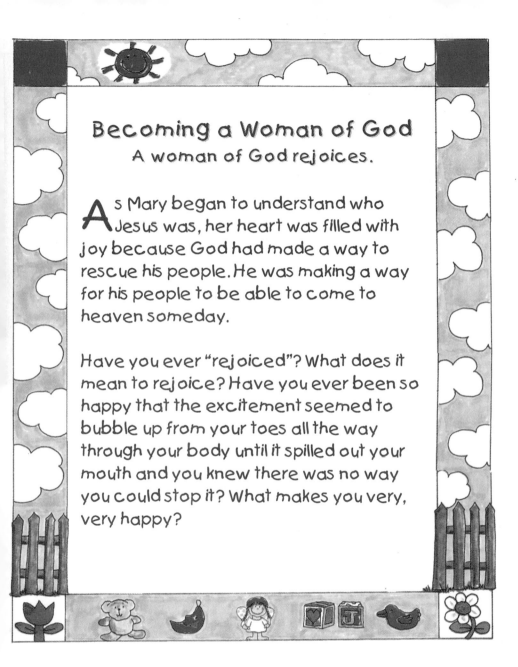

Becoming a Woman of God
A woman of God rejoices.

As Mary began to understand who Jesus was, her heart was filled with joy because God had made a way to rescue his people. He was making a way for his people to be able to come to heaven someday.

Have you ever "rejoiced"? What does it mean to rejoice? Have you ever been so happy that the excitement seemed to bubble up from your toes all the way through your body until it spilled out your mouth and you knew there was no way you could stop it? What makes you very, very happy?

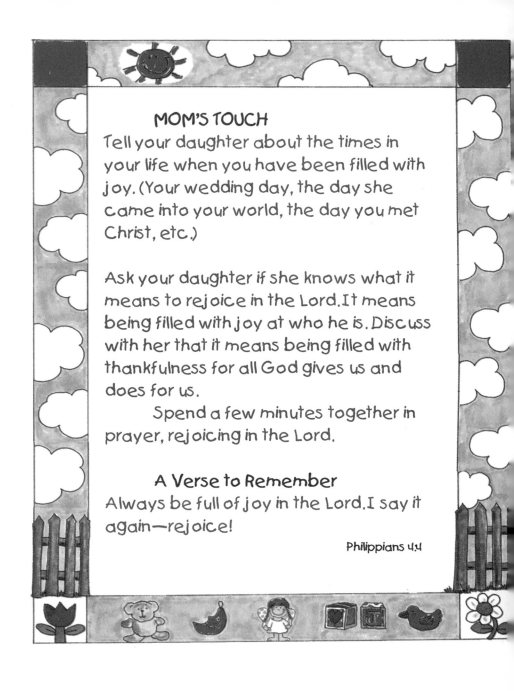

MOM'S TOUCH

Tell your daughter about the times in your life when you have been filled with joy. (Your wedding day, the day she came into your world, the day you met Christ, etc.)

Ask your daughter if she knows what it means to rejoice in the Lord. It means being filled with joy at who he is. Discuss with her that it means being filled with thankfulness for all God gives us and does for us.

Spend a few minutes together in prayer, rejoicing in the Lord.

A Verse to Remember

Always be full of joy in the Lord. I say it again—rejoice!

Philippians 4:4

My Son Is Lost

Mary's side hurt and her lungs felt as if they were going to burst, but she kept running. Joseph was three steps ahead of her as they raced back toward Jerusalem. How on earth did we leave Jesus behind, Mary silently screamed. He's only twelve years old. What will happen to him? She wished her feet would move faster.

"Joseph, this was supposed to be a happy time, it's the Passover ... oh Joseph, what if we can't find him?" Mary cried to her husband.

Joseph waited for her to catch up with him. He hugged her tightly and said, "Trust God, Mary."

"I'm trying," Mary whispered, but her mother's heart cried, "I'm scared."

Mary filled with panic when she saw the crowds in Jerusalem. Why don't these people go home? We have to find our son, her heart cried. Mary and Joseph ran up and down the streets of Jerusalem, stopping people, describing Jesus ... "He's about so tall ... gentle brown eyes. Have you seen him? Please, help us." No one had seen him.

Three days later Mary was exhausted. She didn't think she would ever see Jesus again. "Let's go to the temple and pray for God's help," Joseph suggested. Mary went, but she felt numb inside, like part of her had died. She tried to pray, but the temple was buzzing with people talking about an amazing child who was actually teaching the teachers about God!

A child! It had to be Jesus! Mary and Joseph ran to where a crowd had gathered. Mary's heart flooded with relief when she saw Jesus. Through her sobs she said, "We looked everywhere for you. Why did you do this?"

Jesus was puzzled, "Didn't you know that I would be in my father's house?" He went home with his parents then, and Mary couldn't stop touching his shoulder or brushing his hair back. He's really here. He's safe, her heart sang.

Based on Luke 2:41-52

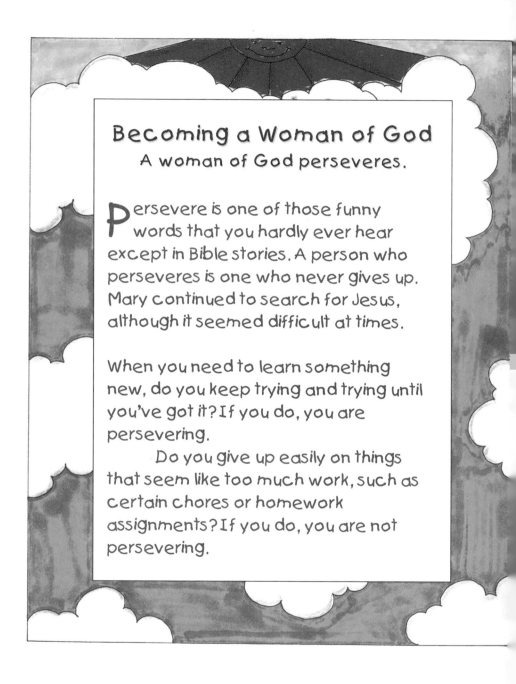

Becoming a Woman of God
A woman of God perseveres.

Persevere is one of those funny words that you hardly ever hear except in Bible stories. A person who perseveres is one who never gives up. Mary continued to search for Jesus, although it seemed difficult at times.

When you need to learn something new, do you keep trying and trying until you've got it? If you do, you are persevering.

Do you give up easily on things that seem like too much work, such as certain chores or homework assignments? If you do, you are not persevering.

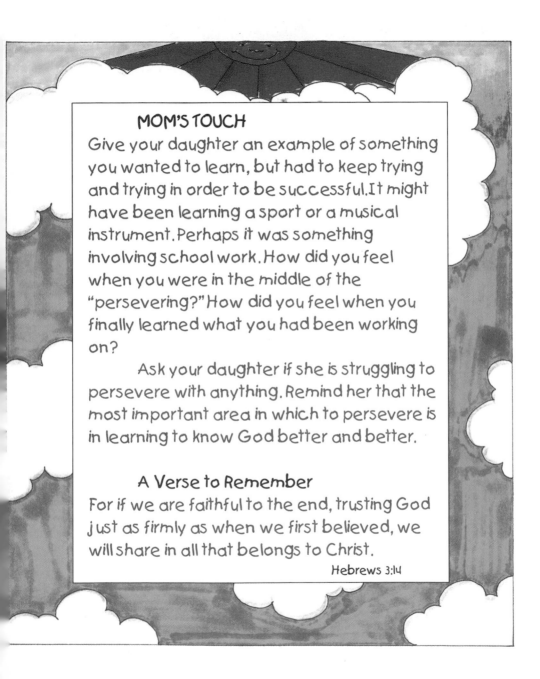

MOM'S TOUCH

Give your daughter an example of something you wanted to learn, but had to keep trying and trying in order to be successful. It might have been learning a sport or a musical instrument. Perhaps it was something involving school work. How did you feel when you were in the middle of the "persevering?" How did you feel when you finally learned what you had been working on?

Ask your daughter if she is struggling to persevere with anything. Remind her that the most important area in which to persevere is in learning to know God better and better.

A Verse to Remember

For if we are faithful to the end, trusting God just as firmly as when we first believed, we will share in all that belongs to Christ.

Hebrews 3:14

An Unusual Wedding Gift

Mary fussed with her hair and smoothed her dress. "I love weddings," she said to no one in particular. "It's so much fun to see old friends and family members. The bride always looks so beautiful and the groom is so handsome. The party after the wedding is so much fun. What a celebration!"

The wedding was as beautiful as Mary had expected. She enjoyed talking with her friends during the party, until she overheard the master of ceremonies talking about a problem. I know who can help, she thought.

"Jesus, the party isn't over, but they've run out of wine," she said to her son.

Jesus calmly answered, "I can't help."

"It's not the time for me to do miracles yet," he continued. Mary stared at him with that look only a mother can give.

Without another word to him, Mary turned to some servants standing nearby, "Do whatever this man tells you to do," she told them.

Jesus then told the servants to fill six big jars with water.

Mary stood off to the side to watch what would happen. The servants filled the jars and brought them back, but Jesus didn't even touch them. He said, "Dip some out and take it to the master of ceremonies."

Mary almost giggled when the man tasted the liquid in the dipper. "This is delicious. It's the best wine I've ever tasted," he cried. The servants' mouths dropped open. They knew they had put water into the jars ... not wine.

Mary looked around for Jesus. He had disappeared into th
crowd after performing this first of many miracles. But his
disciples were talking excitedly among themselves. They
understood now that Jesus was the Son of God.

Mary watched Jesus' disciples grow more and more
excited. She sighed, "Well, it's begun now. Soon the whole
world will know who Jesus is."

Based on John 2:1-11

THE WHOLE WORLD WILL KNOW HIM

Becoming a Woman of God
A woman of God expects great things.

Mary knew that Jesus was the Son of God. She knew that he could do wonderful miracles. She expected him to help the wedding party by doing a miracle. Jesus saw her faith and did his first miracle. Many more followed.

Sometimes "expecting something" is not good—like when you expect your mom or dad to do everything for you, or when you expect your friend to play only with you.

But another kind of "expecting" is when you expect good things to happen. When a woman is going to have a baby, we say she is "expecting." When you're waiting for Grandma and Grandpa to come, you are expecting a visit.

MOM'S TOUCH

Talk with your daughter about a time you "expected" God to do something for you.

When you prayed, did you expect him to answer or did you wonder if he was listening?

Encourage your daughter to believe that God hears her prayers and that he wants to answer. Then she can "expect great things!"

A Verse to Remember

When you ask him, be sure that you really expect him to answer.
James 1:6

The Woman at the Well

The woman walked slowly, her shoulders slumping forward. Life was weighing her down. She appeared to be rather old, but that was just because of the way she carried herself. Bad choices she had made through the years had left her heart empty and hopeless. The sad woman had not felt loved for a long time. She doubted if she would ever be truly loved again.

The woman came to the well alone, carrying a water bucket on her head. Looking up, she noticed a man leaning against the stone well. Ugh! A Jew, she thought. They think they're so much better than us Samaritans. I don't feel like being insulted today, I'll just stay away from him. She went around the well and lowered her bucket into the fresh cool water. She nearly dropped the rope when the man asked her for a drink of water.

"I can't believe you're speaking to me, a lowly Samaritan," she answered sharply. She acted tough to hide the lonely hopelessness inside her. The woman didn't know that this man was Jesus. As they talked, Jesus showed her that he knew many things about her life. At first that made her uncomfortable and she wanted to run away. But as she listened to him, the crust around her heart began to melt.

"God loves you," Jesus said gently. "He wants your worship."

"He can't love me, I've done so many bad things," the woman whispered. "I can't understand this talk about God. I've heard that the Messiah is coming someday. When he comes maybe he can explain it to me."

Jesus looked gently at the woman and said, "I am the Messiah!"

The woman ran back to town shouting at the top of her lungs, "I met the Messiah." Water splashed from her bucket as she grabbed peoples' arms crying, "Come with me, I want you to meet him, too!" She excitedly pulled people to the little well where Jesus waited. Many people believed in Jesus that day because the woman shared the good news she had heard.

Based on John 4:1-42

Becoming a Woman of God
A woman of God shares
the good news.

The woman at the well wasn't a
woman of God until she met Jesus.
When she met him, she wanted to
tell everyone. She wanted everyone
in town to have the same kind of
experience she had just had, so she
called for people to come with her
to meet Jesus.

When you have really great news,
what's the first thing you want to do?
Tell someone, right?
     What great news have you
had? What was the most exciting
thing you ever heard? Who did you
tell?

GOD LOVES YOU......

MOM'S TOUCH

Tell your daughter about the best news you ever got. What was the first thing you did after hearing this news?

Has anyone ever told you good news that they were excited about? What was your reaction to their news? It feels great to have someone celebrate with you, doesn't it?

The best news in the whole world is that God loves us. Tell your daughter about the first person who told you that great news. Ask her who first told her that God loves her. Think together about someone you know who needs to hear that God loves him or her.

A Verse to Remember

This is real love. It is not that we loved God, but that he loved us and sent his Son as a sacrifice to take away our sins.

I John 4:10

Longing To Be Well

"I know he can help me. I've heard of the miracles he does in the name of God. But he's so busy—always surrounded by people who are begging him to do something for them," the sick woman sighed. Jesus and a crowd of people were coming down the road. I don't want to bother Jesus. But I'm sure if I could just touch the hem of his robe, I'd be healed, she thought.

"Well, I've got nothing to lose. The doctors can't help me, and I've been sick so long. This may be my last hope to get well." The woman wiggled and pushed her way through the crowd around Jesus. When she was near him, the woman quietly touched the bottom of Jesus' robe. Instantly she felt her body respond, like a flame shooting through her. "Ohh!" she cried, before clapping a hand over her mouth.

Jesus stopped suddenly and asked, "Who touched me?"

What is he talking about? his disciples wondered. There were hundreds of people around him. Fifty people probably brushed against him in the last five minutes.

But Jesus didn't let the matter drop, "Someone just touched me in order to be healed. I felt power leave me."

The woman shrank back into the crowd and listened to Jesus and his disciples talking. Do I really think I can hide from him? she thought. He's God. I might as well speak up. She meant to be brave, but when she stepped forward she started to shake. In a trembling voice, she said, "I touched you. I've been sick for twelve years and no one could help me. I just wanted to be well, and I knew that I would be if I just touched you."

"When I touched your robe, I was healed..."

The words rolled quickly from her. Everyone was quiet as the woman explained what she had done. But a ripple of shock ran through the crowd when she said, "When I touched your robe, I was healed."

Jesus smiled gently before saying, "Your faith has made you well, my child. Go live your life in peace."

Based on Mark 5:25-34

Becoming a Woman of God
A woman of God steps out in faith.

The woman in this story had a lot of faith. She believed Jesus was so powerful that she could be healed just by touching the hem of his robe. She knew that she didn't need him to touch her or pray for her or even speak to her.

Having faith means that you believe something is true even though you can't see it. When you sit down in a chair and expect it to hold you up and not let you crash to the floor, you are showing faith that the chair will do what it is supposed to do.

MOM'S TOUCH

Tell your daughter about a time when you stepped out in faith to try something. Perhaps your experience relates to a new job or moving to a new state. Tell her how you saw God working in the situation.

Do you or your daughter know anyone who has suffered a long illness, as the woman in the story did? Did that person get depressed and give up hope of ever being better? Discuss this with your daughter.

Encourage your daughter to have faith in God no matter what. We may miss many great blessings in life if we don't have faith in God.

A Verse to Remember

What is faith? It is the confident assurance that what we hope for is going to happen. It is the evidence of things we cannot yet see.

Hebrews 11:1

PAY to the
Order of ____ God ____ $ ♡ ♡ ♡
Giving My All ‿‿‿
Faithful
Praise Him!

The shriveled little woman stood behind a pillar in the temple. She watched as people put their money in the offering box and prayed to God. This is a holy time, she thought. It's a time to praise God for all he has given me. That was an interesting thought, coming from a woman whose husband was dead and who barely had two coins to rub together. Often she didn't even know where her next meal was coming from.

The woman didn't have much family left, most of her loved ones had died. The one most important thing in her life was God. She came to the temple every day to worship and praise him. Now she got in line to give her offering to God. The man ahead of her was dressed in a nice robe with fancy fringe around the edges. He was a rich man who surely had much to be thankful for.

The woman waited with her head bowed. The man made a big show of putting his offering in the box. He made sure everyone was watching. It sounded like a lot of money clinking into the box. The man prayed loudly, but the woman was shocked when she heard him. He didn't praise God at all. Instead, he told God how wonderful he was and how lucky God was that he loved God.

When it was her turn, the poor widow dropped two small coins into the offering box. They didn't make much noise. The two coins together were barely worth a penny. After she put them in the box, the woman bowed her head and praised God for his many wonderful gifts to her. She prayed that her offering would be used to help those who were poorer and needier than she.

The woman didn't notice the rich men standing nearby who were laughing at her. "What a worthless offering. It isn't worth the space it takes up in the box." Just then the woman looked up and saw Jesus standing across the room. He looked deep into the woman's eyes. Jesus knew that this poor woman had given everything she had to God's work. She could see the approval in his eyes. The woman's heart filled with praise and love for God.

Based on Mark 12:41-44

Becoming a Woman of God
A woman of God is humble.

The poor woman was very generous. She gave all that she had to God's work. She knew that it was important to help the needy, and she was willing to give everything for that purpose.

This woman was also very humble. That means that she didn't think more of herself than she should.

Are you humble? Do you know people who are constantly telling everyone how smart they are or how good they are at sports? Do you enjoy being around people who brag about themselves?

MOM'S TOUCH

Tell your daughter about a humble person you have known. Perhaps you have known a missionary who was willing to live in very humble circumstances in order to share God's love with people.

Point out that a humble person doesn't have to own the best of everything, but is happy with what she has. She is willing, as the woman in this story, to give her money, time, talents and energy to the poor. A humble person knows that all she has are gifts from God, so she happily gives back to him.

A Verse to Remember

Don't be selfish; don't live to make a good impression on others. Be humble, thinking of others as better than yourself.

Philippians 2:3

The Gift of Life

"O God, why did you take my son?—my only son?" When her son first got sick the worried mom prayed with all her heart, but the boy still died. The pain in the mother's heart was so great that she could feel nothing else. Her heart was numb. "God, first you took my husband, now my son. It hurts so much. Where are you, God? Where are you?"

Somehow the boy's funeral was planned. She wasn't sure how. She lived from day to day in a fog, hardly aware that friends were around her, or that they were doing things for her. She was grateful for their help, but couldn't even tell them how much it meant to her.

The day of the boy's funeral was warm and sunny, but the heartbroken mother didn't notice the sunshine or feel its warmth on her skin. The funeral procession walked through the town gate and toward the cemetery outside of town. Right outside the gate they met a group of men who had to wait for the procession to pass so they could go into town.

The mother walked slowly behind her son's coffin, her friends trying to comfort her. Suddenly a man's voice said, "Don't cry." The mourners looked at the man as if he were crazy. How could he tell the heartbroken mother not to cry?

The gentle man laid his hand on the boy's coffin. "Young man," he said, "get up!"

Everyone watched as the mother stared at the man in disbelief. When her son sat up, she grabbed her chest, struggling to breathe. Then the grateful woman hugged her son—her only son. She looked up ... into the face of Jesus—God's only Son, and with tears running down her face she praised God for his wonderful love and for giving her back her son.

Based on Luke 7:11-17

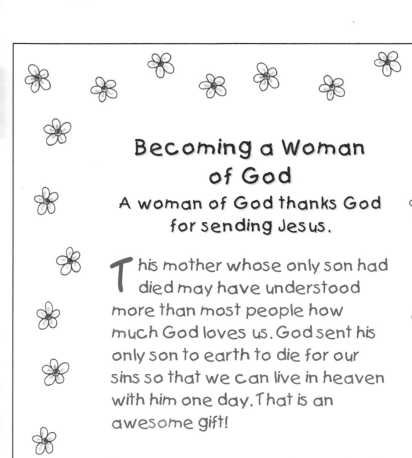

Becoming a Woman of God

A woman of God thanks God for sending Jesus.

This mother whose only son had died may have understood more than most people how much God loves us. God sent his only son to earth to die for our sins so that we can live in heaven with him one day. That is an awesome gift!

Has anyone you loved ever died? Who was it? How did you feel?

MOM'S TOUCH

Tell your little girl how much you love her—and
the entire family. Tell her how you thank God for
your loved ones and for the health and safety
God gives.

    If your family has lost a loved one, talk
about the experience. If that loved one was a
Christian, reinforce that you will see her or him
again one day—in heaven!

    Ask your daughter if she has asked Jesus
to come into her heart. If she hasn't, guide her
through the steps of admitting she has sinned,
asking forgiveness for her sins, and thanking God
for sending Jesus to die for her sins. Then
encourage her to ask Jesus to come live in her
heart forever.

A Verse to Remember

For God so loved the world that he gave his only
Son, so that everyone who believes in him will not
perish but have eternal life.

John 3:16

Daddy's Girl

"Don't worry, Sweetheart. Everything is going to be OK," Jairus told his daughter. The little girl adored her daddy, and believed he could fix anything. For all her twelve years, he had taken care of every problem she ever had. Then one day she got very sick. The little girl was confused because it was the first time her wonderful dad couldn't make everything right.

Her daddy said not to worry. He had heard of a man named Jesus who did wonderful miracles—he healed sick people, and he even brought dead people back to life. Her daddy said he would get Jesus, so she should just rest and wait for him to come back. The little girl believed her daddy because he always did what he said he would do.

She laid back in her bed and rested, confident that her daddy would be back soon with Jesus. She waited and waited, all the while getting sicker and sicker. Her momma stayed beside her and prayed for God to make her well. The little girl tried to hang on. She knew that her daddy would soon be back. But before her daddy could return, the little girl died.

The little girl's momma and grandparents cried and a servant ran to tell Jairus that it was too late—his precious little girl was dead. When Jairus heard the news, he sadly turned and started home. But Jesus insisted on coming with him, even though the girl was dead.

Later, Jairus held his little girl and told her how people had laughed when Jesus said she wasn't dead, but that she was just sleeping. But then Jesus had taken her hand and said, "Get up, little girl," and she did!

The little girl loved hearing the story and asked to hear it over and over again. Jairus always ended the story by hugging her and thanking God for giving his daughter back to him.

Based on Mark 5:22-24, 35-43

Becoming a Woman of God
A woman of God thanks God for second chances.

Jairus' daughter was given a second chance at life. If you were Jairus' daughter wouldn't you want to hear the story over and over? That experience may have changed how she looked at life.

Have you ever been given a second chance? Maybe when you disobeyed, Mom and Dad forgave you and gave you a second chance. What about at school? Maybe you did poorly on an exam, and you were given a chance to retake it.

Life is filled with second chances. A wise person understands that and makes the most of the second chance.

MOM'S TOUCH

How do you feel when your daughter disobeys? How about when she breaks the same rule over and over? Share your feelings with your daughter.

Can you remember a time when you were given a second chance at something? How did you respond? Explain to your daughter how you felt about the person who gave you the second chance.

Ask your daughter how she feels when you give her a second chance. Remind her that God will give us a second chance when we confess our sins and ask for his forgiveness.

A Verse to Remember

If we confess our sins to him, he is faithful and just to forgive us and to cleanse us from every wrong.

I John 1:9

A Mother's Love

A mother's love is just about the strongest thing in the
world, but this mother's love had nearly reached its limit.
She never knew when her daughter was going to explode
in anger or act downright mean. Sometimes with no
warning her precious little girl would act like a monster.
The demon living inside the girl made her do whatever it
wanted. It was so frustrating.

The poor woman felt helpless. She had tried everything she could think of to help her daughter. But nothing worked. The woman wasn't Jewish, but she had heard of a Jewish man named Jesus who taught his people about God. He healed the sick, brought dead people back to life, and even chased demons out of people. It can't hurt to ask for Jesus' help. I've got nothing to lose. All he can do is say no, she thought.

I'll ask Jesus to help me.

So, the desperate woman went looking for Jesus. When she found him, she hid behind a tree and watched him for a while. He didn't look scary. If anything he seemed kind and loving. So, filled with the power of a mother's love, she marched up to him and asked, "Jesus, please help my daughter. There's a demon inside her and it is driving her crazy. Please, help her."

Jesus didn't say a word. The woman was dying inside, wondering if he was angry. His disciples finally broke the silence. "Send this Gentile away. Her begging is getting on our nerves."

The woman wanted to shout, "My daughter and I are people. We have problems the same as you Jews do." But she didn't say a word.

She had nearly given up when Jesus finally spoke, "I came to help the Jews, not the Gentiles."

The woman dropped to her knees and begged for his help.

But Jesus answered, "Helping a Gentile would be like taking food from children and giving it to dogs."

She had an answer. "Yes, but even dogs sit under the table and eat the crumbs that fall on the floor."

A smile tugged at Jesus' mouth, "Your faith is strong so I have done what you asked." The woman hurried home and found that the demon was gone. She told her daughter what Jesus had done and together they praised God.

Based on Matthew 15:21-28

Becoming a Woman of God
A woman of God is concerned about others.

This woman was concerned about her daughter. She didn't really know if Jesus would help her or tell her to go away. She was willing to do anything for her child. She risked rejection and embarrassment.

A woman who loves God also loves others and shows concern for other people.

Have you observed someone showing concern for others? How did it happen? Did that person risk being embarrassed or rejected in order to help someone else?

MOM'S TOUCH

Tell about a time when your mother or caregiver showed real concern for you. What was the situation? How did this person show concern? How did you feel about that person then?

Have you observed your daughter showing concern for others? Praise her for that concern.

Think together of ways you both can show concern for others.

A Verse to Remember

There are three things that will endure—faith, hope, and love—and the greatest of these is love.

I Corinthians 13:13

A Gracious Hostess

All through Martha's childhood her mother said she was a worrier. Martha couldn't help it. She worried and fussed because everything had to be perfect ... especially when they had company. There couldn't be a speck of dust in the whole house, the table had to be set beautifully with fresh flowers, and dinner had to be ready exactly on time. Martha simply couldn't settle for anything less.

There couldn't be two more opposite people than Martha and her sister. Martha was a "doer" while Mary was a "thinker". Mary could be gone for hours, smelling flowers, watching birds, or chatting with merchants. When they had guests for dinner, Mary got so involved in talking to them that she'd forget to help Martha serve the meal. This wasn't a problem for Mary, but Martha was often very frustrated with her sister.

When the sisters heard that Jesus was coming to visit, there was a flurry of busyness ...from Martha. She cleaned and cooked and washed and worked right up to the minute Jesus came. Martha made a wonderful dinner, and she thought Mary would surely help with the final preparations. But as soon as Jesus came in, Mary sat down right at his feet to listen to his wonderful stories. Martha stomped off to the kitchen in a huff.

Martha scurried around the kitchen, mixing, stirring, and chopping. Every few minutes she peeked around the door, hoping Mary was coming to help. She wasn't. In fact, each time Martha looked, Mary seemed to be deeper in conversation with Jesus. Pretty soon, Martha was steaming mad, "I work my fingers to the bone to clean the house and prepare a wonderful dinner and Mary just sits out there talking to him," she thought. "It isn't fair!"

Martha was so angry that she began slamming things around the kitchen. Finally, she could take it no longer. Marching in to Jesus, she said, "Tell her to get up and help me. I'd like to hear your stories, too, but someone has to cook dinner."

Jesus was surprised at Martha's anger. Mary didn't dare say a word, but Jesus said, "Martha, you're so upset about your work. But, Mary knows that talking to me is more important than anything. Forget the kitchen, let's talk."

Based on Luke 10:38-42

Becoming a Woman of God
A woman of God knows what's most important.

Martha had good intentions. After all, she was busy doing what she was good at. It was important to her to have the house clean for Jesus' visit and to serve him a good meal.

But, even though she meant well, Martha let her work keep her so busy that she missed the most important thing—spending time with Jesus.

Nothing should be more important than spending time with Jesus. Even if God has given you some special talents that you can use in church, such as singing or playing an instrument, those talents should never get in the way of spending time with God.

MOM'S TOUCH

Have you ever gotten so busy "doing things"
that you let slide the really important things in
life? Things like spending time daily with God, or
spending time with your family? It's easy for
that to happen in our busy world. Talk to your
daughter about your struggle between the
"urgent" and the "important."

Tell her some ways you try to make room
for what's really important. Then help her plan
a daily schedule that includes quiet time with
God.

A Verse to Remember

Love the LORD your God, walk in all his ways,
obey his commands, be faithful to him, and
serve him with all your heart and all your soul.

Joshua 22:5

Lazarus, Come Out!

Mary choked back tears as she poured spices on Lazarus' body. Martha was doing most of the work to prepare their brother for burial. She didn't act sad at all, but Mary knew she was. Working hard was Martha's way of handling her pain. Suddenly, Mary felt tired. She sat down and thought back to when she, Martha, and Lazarus were children.

A smile tugged at Mary's mouth as she remembered how Lazarus loved to tease. "Mary, I know it's hard, but we must finish," Martha gently interrupted.

"Aren't you tired, Martha?" Mary asked.

"Yes, I am tired . . . and disappointed that Jesus didn't come," Martha sighed. "He could have helped Lazarus. There, I've said it."

Mary sighed. She was disappointed, too.

The sisters had sent for Jesus when Lazarus had gotten sick. They were sure he would come and heal their brother. But he didn't, and Lazarus had died.

After Lazarus was buried, Mary and Martha went home. Many relatives and friends came to comfort them. A few days later someone shouted, "Jesus is coming."

Martha dropped the dough she was kneading and ran to meet him. "My brother is dead," she told him. "If you had come when we sent for you, he would still be alive."

"Martha, those who believe in me are given eternal life. They will never die. Do you believe that?"

"Yes," Martha said, "I know you are the Son of God."

Mary came to see Jesus too. She also said that Lazarus would have lived if Jesus had come sooner. She could barely speak through her choking sobs.

"Where is Lazarus buried?" Jesus asked. Tears were crawling down his face, too. Mary and Martha showed him the tomb, a cave with a big stone covering the opening.

"Move the stone," Jesus ordered. Martha was shocked, "No, the smell will be awful. He has been dead four days!"

"Watch what God will do," Jesus answered. Martha grabbed Mary's hand, and they watched Jesus. He looked up and prayed. Then he called, "Lazarus, come out!" Mary closed her eyes, but Martha didn't. When Martha gasped and squeezed her hand, Mary opened one eye. A man was standing in the cave's door, wrapped in graveclothes. Lazarus was alive!

Based on John 11:1-45

Becoming a Woman of God
A woman of God believes in the resurrection of believers.

Jesus taught an important lesson here to Mary and Martha. People who believe in him know that they will live forever. They may die on this earth, but they will be alive in heaven forever (with him!).

This is a wonderful promise for people who believe in Jesus. No matter what happens in this life, no matter how difficult things get, we know that one day we will be in heaven with him. Praise God!

The idea of becoming alive again after we have died is hard to understand, isn't it? What do you think heaven will be like?

MOM'S TOUCH

Share with your daughter what you know about heaven. Talk about how you feel when you think about seeing loved ones there who have already died.

Explain how this promise is one of the reasons there is an urgency to share God's love with all those around you. We all want our friends and family members to be with us in heaven someday.

Discuss someone you and your daughter both know who doesn't know about Jesus. Can you think of a way to share God's love with that person?

A Verse to Remember

I am the resurrection and the life. Those who believe in me, even though they die like everyone else, will live again.

John 11:25

Miracle of Mud

She was his mother. If she could have changed things, she would have. When her son was born blind, of course she prayed, "Take my eyesight, just let my son see." She tried everything that doctors suggested. She wondered what she could have done differently when she was pregnant or even if he was blind because of a sin she or her husband had committed. But he remained blind. Now he was a blind man who could only beg to earn his living.

One afternoon a crowd of Pharisees showed up, dragging her son with them. Someone shouted, "Is this your son? Wasn't he born blind?" She started to answer, but he shouted again, "How come he can see now?"

Her heart leaped into her throat. He can see? After all these years, he can see? She looked at her son and realized that he was seeing her—for the very first time.

She wanted to hug him, ask him what happened, but the Pharisees kept shouting, "Why can he see now?"

Her husband came out and together they faced the crowd, "Yes, this is our son. Yes, he was born blind. We don't know why he can see now. He's an adult, ask him."

The confused parents listened as their son explained, "Jesus spit on the ground and made mud. Then he smeared the mud on my eyes. I didn't know what he was doing, but when he told me to wash off the mud in the pool of Siloam, I did. As soon as I did, I could see!"

The worried mother twisted her scarf in her hands. Son, she thought, be careful, these men don't like Jesus. They'll be angry that you're giving him credit for this. The Pharisees leaned right into her son's face. She wanted to yank them back, but they kept asking, "How did he heal you?"

"Why do you keep asking me?" her son sighed. "I told you everything he did!"

Oh my, she worried, they're going to throw him in jail. But just then Jesus himself walked up. She couldn't take her eyes off Jesus. He was a gentle man, but somehow power and authority flowed from him. He turned to her son and asked, "Do you believe in the son of Man?"

The woman's heart sang as she saw her grown-up son fall to his knees and worship Jesus, "I believe," he said.

Based on John 9:1-41

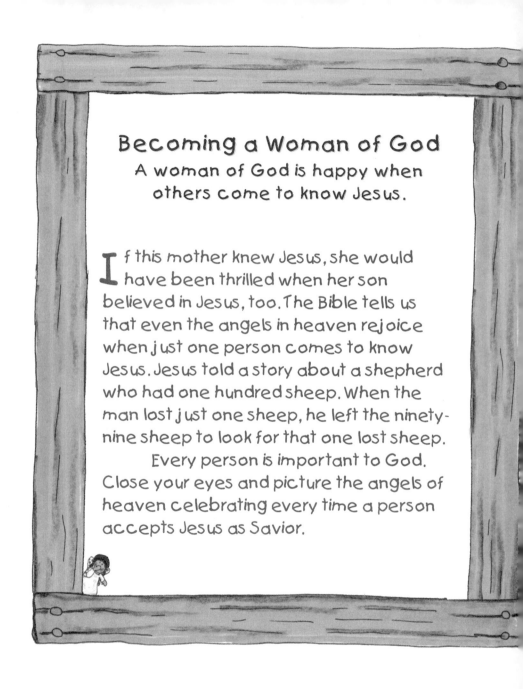

Becoming a Woman of God
A woman of God is happy when others come to know Jesus.

If this mother knew Jesus, she would have been thrilled when her son believed in Jesus, too. The Bible tells us that even the angels in heaven rejoice when just one person comes to know Jesus. Jesus told a story about a shepherd who had one hundred sheep. When the man lost just one sheep, he left the ninety-nine sheep to look for that one lost sheep.

Every person is important to God. Close your eyes and picture the angels of heaven celebrating every time a person accepts Jesus as Savior.

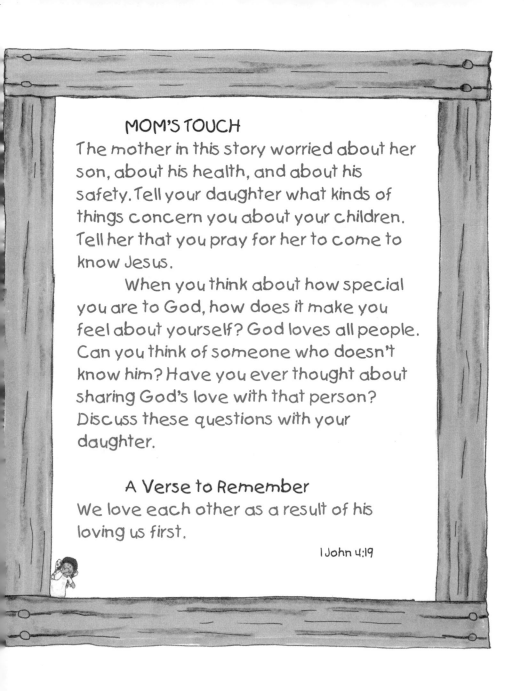

MOM'S TOUCH

The mother in this story worried about her son, about his health, and about his safety. Tell your daughter what kinds of things concern you about your children. Tell her that you pray for her to come to know Jesus.

When you think about how special you are to God, how does it make you feel about yourself? God loves all people. Can you think of someone who doesn't know him? Have you ever thought about sharing God's love with that person? Discuss these questions with your daughter.

A Verse to Remember

We love each other as a result of his loving us first.

I John 4:19

A Gift of Love

The woman stood across the street watching men go into Simon's house. When it seemed that all of Simon's guests had arrived, the woman crept a little closer and peeked in an open window. The wonderful smell of expensive food drifted out, finer food than she had ever eaten. The men in the room were talking and laughing.

Her eyes roamed through the room until she found the one face for which she was searching. Jesus. The woman dared to lean even closer for a better look at him. Her heart filled with love for this gentle man. She had met him once before, and he had chased away the demons that haunted her days and nights, giving her a chance for a normal life.

The woman was so overwhelmed with love for
Jesus that she did something many would consider
foolish. Hurrying to her shabby home she took a
beautiful alabastar jar from her cupboard. It was
filled with priceless perfume, more special than
anything else she owned and worth more money
than all her other possessions put together. She was
going to give it away.

She wrapped the priceless jar in a cloth and hurried back to Simon's house. She wasn't welcome in his home because most people didn't approve of her lifestyle. The woman stopped at the door and took a deep breath before barging in. She went to Jesus and knelt at his feet.

The room became very quiet as the men watched tears run down the woman's face and fall on Jesus' feet. She gently wiped them away with her hair.

A loud gasp rolled through the room when she broke open the jar and poured the priceless perfume on Jesus' feet.

Simon criticized Jesus for letting such a woman touch him, but the woman's heart filled with love for Jesus when he defended her. She had so much to be thankful for because Jesus had forgiven her for so much.

Now he gently lifted her to her feet and said, "Your faith has saved you; go in peace."

Based on Luke 7:36-50

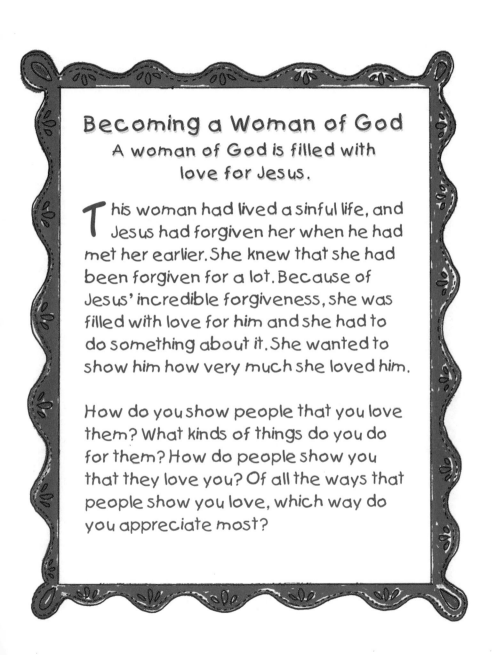

Becoming a Woman of God
A woman of God is filled with love for Jesus.

This woman had lived a sinful life, and Jesus had forgiven her when he had met her earlier. She knew that she had been forgiven for a lot. Because of Jesus' incredible forgiveness, she was filled with love for him and she had to do something about it. She wanted to show him how very much she loved him.

How do you show people that you love them? What kinds of things do you do for them? How do people show you that they love you? Of all the ways that people show you love, which way do you appreciate most?

MOM'S TOUCH

Tell your daughter what expressions of love you most appreciate, from her and from others. Tell her how you like to show her and others that you love them. Give her ideas for ways to show people that she loves them.

Discuss with your daughter some of the ways we can show God we love him. Remind her to look for ways to show her friends that she loves God . . . and that he loves them.

A Verse to Remember

You must love the Lord your God with all your heart, all your soul, and all your mind.

Matthew 22:37

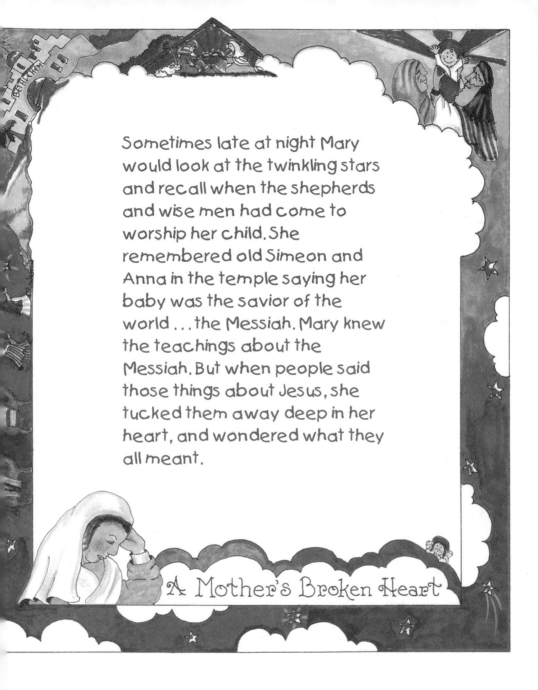

Sometimes late at night Mary would look at the twinkling stars and recall when the shepherds and wise men had come to worship her child. She remembered old Simeon and Anna in the temple saying her baby was the savior of the world ... the Messiah. Mary knew the teachings about the Messiah. But when people said those things about Jesus, she tucked them away deep in her heart, and wondered what they all meant.

A Mother's Broken Heart

Today, she knew what they meant . . . and her heart was breaking. With every ounce of her being, Mary wanted to run through the streets of Jerusalem shouting, "Don't hurt him. He's my son. God, do something—STOP THEM!" Yet deep in her heart, she knew that the events of this day could not be stopped. Mary stood in the crowd as Jesus struggled to carry the heavy wooden cross. The cross on which he would die.

Mary was swept along with the crowd to the hill called Golgotha. She slid to the back of the crowd when the soldiers threw Jesus to the ground and began pounding the heavy spikes through his hands and feet and into the wooden cross. With every clank of the hammer, Mary wanted to turn and run as far away from this horrible scene as possible, but she couldn't. He was her son, and she had to stay with him.

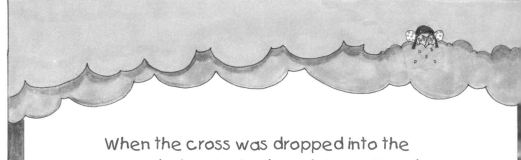

When the cross was dropped into the
ground, Mary looked up at Jesus. Blood was
running down his face, mixed with the
sweat of agonizing pain. She looked into his
eyes, the same eyes she had played hide
and seek with when he was a toddler, eyes
that had laughingly teased her when he
was a child, gentle eyes that even on this
most horrible of days were filled with love
for the sinful people who had come to
watch him die.

Mary's eyes were locked on Jesus, wishing she could send strength from her body to his. She knew the end was near when Jesus asked one of his friends to take care of her and she felt an arm slip around her shoulder.

When Jesus died, Mary fell to her knees, sobbing in agony. "My arms feel so empty, I ache to hold my son, to tell him that everything will be alright." Simeon's long ago words made sense now. Her soul was pierced by the pain of this moment.

Based on John 19:1-30

Becoming a Woman of God
A woman of God understands
Jesus' sacrifice.

On the day that Jesus died, Mary was very sad. It wasn't fair that the Son of God and the savior of the world was dying on a cross. It made Mary's heart break. It might have been easy for Mary to forget that this horrible moment was part of God's big plan to save mankind.

Jesus left heaven to come to earth and live as a poor man. He was treated badly by the very people he came to save. And he was killed as if he were a murderer. He did all of this because of his great love for us.

How do you feel when you are blamed for something you did not do?

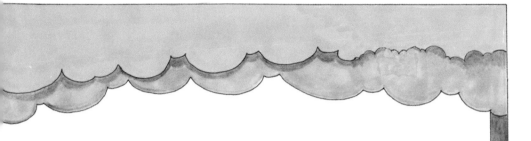

MOM'S TOUCH

There isn't an emotion much more intense than a mother's love. Tell your daughter about a time when she was sick or hurting and you hurt right along with her.

In the Old Testament, people had to sacrifice an animal, such as a sheep, to God in order ask for the forgiveness of their sins. Talk to your daughter about what Jesus went through because he loved us. Jesus' death on the cross is the sacrifice for our sin. When we confess our sins, and accept Jesus' sacrifice, he will come live in our hearts forever.

A Verse to Remember

Believe on the Lord Jesus and you will be saved.

Acts 16:31

A New Day Dawns

The three women got up early Sunday morning,
before the sun rose. Their hearts were heavy with
pain. The man they had believed in with all their
hearts was gone ... dead. Each of the women was
lost in her own thoughts: I thought he was the
one—the Messiah. How can he be dead? I kept
waiting for him to call an army of angels to rescue
him from that horrible cross, but he didn't. He didn't.
And now he's dead.

Even in the middle of their pain and confusion the women wanted to do what was right. So they gathered spices and perfumes to put on his body. It was their custom to do this after a person had died. But there hadn't been time on the day he died because it was too close to the Sabbath. At first the women walked along in silence, each lost in her own sad thoughts.

How can we move it?

But as they neared the tomb, one woman spoke. Her practical question broke through the fog of grief surrounding each of them. "How are we going to move the stone?" The women stopped and looked at each other. It was overwhelming. They had been through so much in the last few days and they were exhausted. "How are we going to move the huge stone that covers the tomb door?" the woman repeated her question.

The women were still worried about the stone when they reached the cave. Then the first woman shouted, "It's gone. The stone is gone— the tomb is open." They stared at the gaping doorway, more confused than ever.

Suddenly, an angel stood in front of them. "I know you're looking for Jesus," the angel said. "He isn't here. He came back to life, just as he said he would. Hurry to town and tell his friends."

For a split second the women stood in silence, letting the angel's news sink in. Then they exploded with joy. They went from deep, deep pain to incredible joy so quickly that their hearts had trouble keeping up. "He's alive!" they shouted, running to the disciples. "He's alive. Just as he said, he has come back to life!"

Based on Luke 24:1-12

Becoming a Woman of God
A woman of God has hope.

These women thought all hope was gone. They thought all their hope had died with Jesus. So the angel's announcment that Jesus was alive again brought hope back to their hearts.

Hope helps us through the hard times. If we believe that Jesus is alive, we share the same hope that the women in this story had.

Have you ever hoped for something? What was it? Did it happen? How did you feel then?

MOM'S TOUCH

Share some of your hopes with your daughter. Hopes for the future, hopes for her future. Share some of the hopes you had when you were a young adult, just beginning the journey of adulthood and parenthood.

Remind your daughter that the truth of Jesus' resurrection gives us great hope for the future. Because Jesus is alive, we know that we will be in heaven with him someday.

Thank Jesus together for the wonderful hope of being in heaven with him!

A Verse to Remember

O Lord, you alone are my hope. I've trusted you, O LORD, from childhood.

Psalm 71:5

Mary Magdalene couldn't leave. The disciples had gone back to town, convinced that Jesus had risen from the dead. But Mary couldn't bring herself to leave the tomb. It was all too confusing. Had he really come back to life? If not, where was his body? Had someone stolen it as a cruel joke?

When Jesus died on Friday, it was the darkest day of Mary's life. He was such a pure and holy man and she didn't understand why anyone would hurt him. She wanted more than anything to believe that he was truly alive. But there had been so many disappointments in the last few days, she was afraid to believe this time. So she sat beside the tomb, crying. After a while, she ducked inside the tomb for one last lonely look around.

The cave suddenly filled with light and Mary looked up to see two beautiful angels, "Why are you crying?" they asked.

"Because someone has taken Jesus away, and I don't know where he is," she said. The angels left and Mary came out into the sunlight feeling an unbearable sense of loss.

Sinking down on a rock, Mary thought about things she wished she had told him. Jesus had forgiven her when she hadn't been able to forgive herself. I wish I had another chance to tell him how much that meant, she thought.

As Mary started to leave, she saw a man standing nearby. "Sir, are you the gardener? Did you take Jesus' body away?" Words spilled from Mary's lips. "Tell me where you put him. I'll get him."

"Mary."

Wait, something was familiar. Mary stared at the man until the fog in her brain lifted and she realized, "It's Jesus!" Bursting into tears she rushed to hug him and whisper all the words that had been flooding her heart.

But Jesus gently stopped her, "You can't touch me yet, Mary. Tell my friends that I'm going back to my Father—to your Father." Mary cried with joy as she left for town, knowing that everything would be all right now.

Based on John 20:10-18

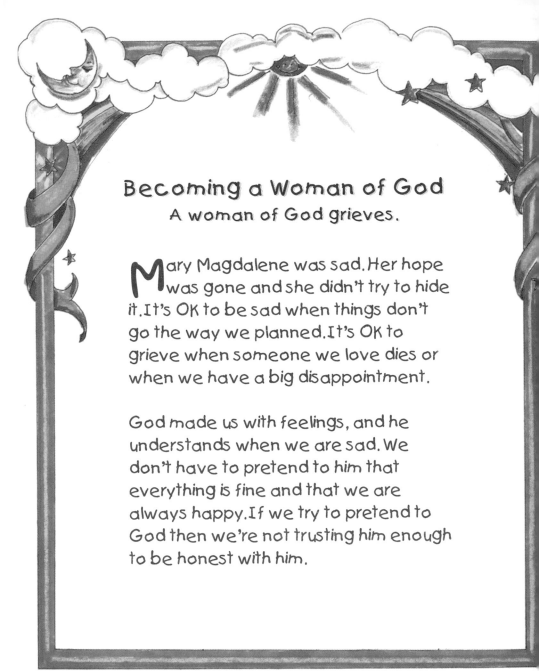

Becoming a Woman of God
A woman of God grieves.

Mary Magdalene was sad. Her hope was gone and she didn't try to hide it. It's OK to be sad when things don't go the way we planned. It's OK to grieve when someone we love dies or when we have a big disappointment.

God made us with feelings, and he understands when we are sad. We don't have to pretend to him that everything is fine and that we are always happy. If we try to pretend to God then we're not trusting him enough to be honest with him.

MOM'S TOUCH

Has your daughter ever seen you grieve? If mothers never show their pain, daughters will have difficulty learning how to handle theirs. One gift we can give our children is to show them that it's OK to be sad. Even Jesus was sad sometimes.

Tell your daughter about a sad time you went through. How did God help you? Ask her to tell you about one of her sad times. Talk about what kinds of things make you sad. Talk about what makes you happy. Mary Magdalene experienced both sadness and joy very close together!

A Verse to Remember

Truly, you will weep and mourn over what is going to happen to me, but the world will rejoice. You will grieve, but your grief will suddenly turn to wonderful joy when you see me again.

John 16:20

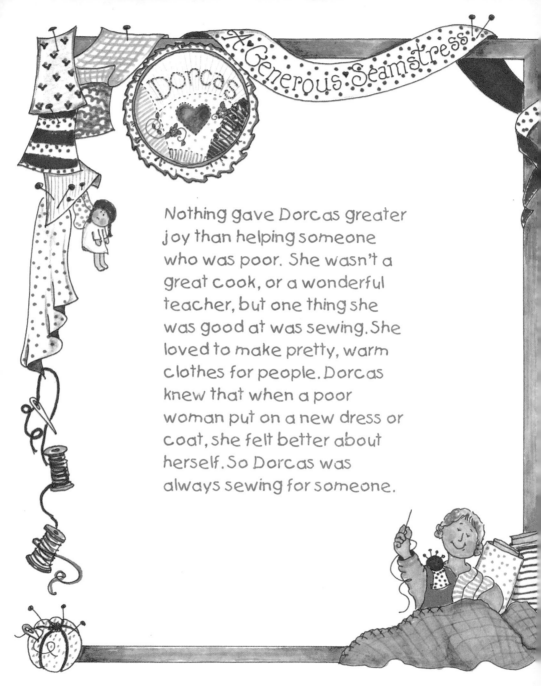

A Generous Seamstress

Dorcas

Nothing gave Dorcas greater joy than helping someone who was poor. She wasn't a great cook, or a wonderful teacher, but one thing she was good at was sewing. She loved to make pretty, warm clothes for people. Dorcas knew that when a poor woman put on a new dress or coat, she felt better about herself. So Dorcas was always sewing for someone.

When Dorcas started feeling sick, her friends tried to
get her to slow down. "Take some time off. You've
earned it. Take a rest," they told her. But Dorcas kept
stitching away. There was always one more person who
could use a new robe or dress. Dorcas wouldn't let
herself slow down.

Her friends noticed that Dorcas was getting weaker and weaker. Her stitches weren't as even as before and her fingers weren't flying across the fabric. "Please Dorcas, stop and rest," they pleaded.

But she wouldn't. "The good Lord gave me a gift, and I'm going to use it." A few days later, Dorcas' friends found her dead, with her sewing needle still in her hands.

Dorcas' friends cried as they put perfumes on her body and dressed her in a nice dress. It was sad that such a giving person was gone. Many people would miss her.

Then someone mentioned that Peter was nearby. "God has helped Peter do wonderful miracles. He has even raised people from the dead," someone added. "Let's send for him. Maybe he will help Dorcas!"

When Peter came, Dorcas' friends sadly showed him the clothing she had made for them. Peter sent them all out of the room. Then he prayed and took Dorcas by the hand. "Get up," he ordered. Her eyes fluttered open and breath swooshed back into her body. Dorcas sat up, alive and well! Peter called her friends to come back in. They all joyfully praised God for giving Dorcas back to them.

Based on Acts 9:36-43

Becoming a Woman of God
A woman of God helps others.

Dorcas loved helping others by doing what she was best at— sewing. Dorcas really cared about people. So she helped them in the best way that she could.

Since Dorcas cared so much for others, she had many friends. Loving people are usually surrounded by friends.

Do you like to help other people? What do you enjoy doing that might be a way to show others that you care about them?

MOM'S TOUCH

Discuss with your daughter a time when someone helped you in some way. What did that person do for you? Did it make you feel as if that person cared about you?

Think out loud with your daughter about ways that the two of you can help others. What do you both enjoy doing? How can you show people that you care about them?

A Verse to Remember

This is the message we have heard from the beginning: We should love one another.

I John 3:11

Lydia's days were busy with selling the purple dye for which her home town of Thyatira was famous. The business was going well and she was thankful that she didn't have to worry about money or food. When the Sabbath came, she could have used the time to rest. After all, she wasn't Jewish. But, on the Sabbath day Lydia would gather with a small group of women on the banks of the river outside town.

One bright Sabbath morning, the women had gathered on the quiet river banks when a man's voice interrupted their conversation. Lydia looked up at the two men and was shocked to recognize the apostle Paul. He traveled all around the country teaching people about God. What is Paul doing here, on a damp riverbank with a bunch of women? she thought. It wasn't long before Lydia knew.

Paul sat down with the women. He prayed with them and began teaching them about Jesus' death and resurrection and God's incredible plan. Lydia listened as Paul explained God's wonderful love. She had worshiped God but had never really understood him until now. It seemed to Lydia as if God opened a window in her heart for just a moment, and, suddenly everything made sense.

Joyfully, Lydia asked Jesus to be her Lord and Savior.
"Would you baptize me right now?" she asked Paul.
They stepped into the river and Lydia said she
believed in Jesus. Then Paul lowered her down into
the water. When he lifted her out of the water, Lydia
knew in her heart that she was a new person and her
life would never be the same.

Lydia wanted to run into town and tell everyone, to shout her new faith from the rooftops. She was also eager to share all that she had. Turning to Paul, Lydia said, "You must come stay at my house. Please, bring your friends. I have plenty of room. If you really believe that I'm a Christian now, please come." Paul laughed at Lydia's enthusiasm and happily accepted her hospitality.

Based on Acts 16:11-15

Becoming a Woman of God
A woman of God is God's friend.

Lydia was introduced to a personal relationship with God by the apostle Paul. As soon as she met God, what did she want to do? She wanted to do something nice for Paul. She invited him to stay at her house.

When Lydia became God's friend, she probably wanted to know more and more about God. Perhaps that's why she wanted Paul to stay at her house—so she could talk with him more.

The best way to become friends with someone is to spend time with that person and get to know all you can about that person.

MOM'S TOUCH

Tell your daughter about one of your close friends. Why are you and your friend so close? Do you have the same interests or hobbies? Do you have the same kinds of personalities? Has your friend ever done something nice for you? What was it? What kinds of things do you do for your friend?

Ask your daughter to describe her best friend.

Now encourage your daughter in her friendship with God. Discuss how we get to know God and how we stay in touch with him. Encourage her to schedule a time with God every day.

A Verse to Remember

Keep on praying.

I Thessalonians 5:17

Priscilla and her husband Aquila were tentmakers. It was a good living, but the work was hard. One good thing was that they met a lot of people. Priscilla enjoyed the end of the day when all the workers would sit around and share stories. One fellow they met was a man named Paul. Paul talked about Jesus. He explained how Jesus died and came back to life and that after he went back to heaven he sent the Holy Spirit to help Christians.

SHARING WHAT YOU KNOW

Priscilla learned a lot from Paul, but sometimes what Paul said made her feel that she wasn't doing her part in spreading the good news about God. She and Aquila promised each other to be more brave about sharing their faith in God with others. They could tell their customers and even other tentmakers.

One time when Priscilla and Aquila were working in Ephesus, they heard a man teaching about God. It was exciting to hear another person teaching about the faith. Priscilla walked a little closer and listened to Apollos for a while and then came back to talk to her husband.

"Aquila," she said, "Apollos is teaching about John's baptism, but he doesn't know the rest of the story—the things that Paul taught us. He doesn't know about Jesus' death and resurrection. He doesn't know about the Holy Spirit. We have to tell him, Aquila. We know the whole story, and we should tell him."

"Why didn't you just go up and tell him?" Aquila asked.

"I didn't want to embarrass him in front of the people he was teaching," Priscilla said. "Let's invite him over for dinner, and we'll talk to him privately."

So Priscilla and Aquila invited Apollos over and privately told him the rest of the wonderful story. Now he could teach the entire truth about God's loving plan.

Based on Acts 18:18-28; Romans 16:3

Becoming a Woman of God
A woman of God is sensitive to others' feelings.

We don't really know why Priscilla didn't talk to Apollos in front of other people, but maybe she was being sensitive. She might have thought that it would make him feel bad if she talked to him in front of other people, or that the people would stop listening to his teaching.

How do you feel about someone who embarrasses you on purpose? It's not nice to feel that someone wants to hurt you.

How do you feel about friends who are careful not to embarrass you, but talk to you privately if they have a problem with something you're doing?

MOM'S TOUCH

Being embarrassed in front of friends is just about the worst thing that can happen to a young person. Did it ever happen to you? Describe the situation to your daughter and tell her how you handled it. How did you feel about the person who embarrassed you?

Now look at the other side. Describe a person who was sensitive to your feelings. Did you feel more kindly toward that person? Talk together about ways you can both be sensitive to other people. How can you both show people that you care about their feelings?

A Verse to Remember

Do for others what you would like them to do for you.

Matthew 7:12

An Angel at the door

Rhoda was a servant girl, so it was a bit of an honor for her to join the Christians' worship service. Tonight was a special prayer service for Peter. Rhoda liked Peter although she was too shy to talk to the loud fisherman. He told wonderful stories that made her laugh.

Peter was in prison. He might even be killed, so the situation was serious. Rhoda found it confusing because Peter's only crime was that he was a Christian.

A soft rumble filled the room as groups of people huddled together, praying for Peter's safety. Rhoda sat in a group near the door. In her heart she prayed as earnestly for Peter as everyone else did, but she was too shy to pray out loud. Sometime late in the evening there was a knock on the door. Rhoda tried to ignore it and concentrate on praying. But the knocking got louder and louder.

Rhoda noticed that the noise was bothering other people, so she went to see who was at the door. When she opened the peek hole, Rhoda couldn't believe who was standing outside. "Rhoda, let me in," Peter said.

Rhoda screamed and ran into the room of praying people. "It's Peter! Peter is at the door!" she shouted.

But noone believed Rhoda, "It can't be Peter. It must be his angel—he must already be dead!" Then the knocking turned to pounding, and all eyes looked at Rhoda. So, once again she went to the door. But this time she remembered to let Peter come in. Every person in the room stood and cheered when Peter walked in.

Peter gave Rhoda a little hug before he began explaining how God had sent an angel to lead him out of the prison. Rhoda listened to Peter's wonderful story of how God had miraculously freed him. Rhoda joined the others as they happily shouted, "Praise God!"

Based on Acts 12:12-17

Becoming a Woman of God
A woman of God serves others.

Rhoda was a servant girl. Her job was to do things for other people or help others with the jobs they had to do.

Sometimes people think that a sign of real success in life is to have people who will do your jobs for you— someone to clean your house, do your yardwork, or even drive your car for you. But Jesus showed by the way he lived, and what he taught, that children of God should serve others, not be served.

MOM'S TOUCH

Share with your daughter a time when someone served you by doing something for you without being asked. How did you feel about that person? After that experience, how did you feel about doing things for other people?

Talk with your daughter about how she can share God's love with others by serving them. Talk about ways she can serve other people. Remind her that it's important to have a humble attitude and not demand praise for serving others.

A Verse to Remember

For even I, the Son of Man, came here not to be served but to serve others, and to give my life as a ransom for many.

Matthew 20:28